May the 1...
this book always
lift your spirit

Twila Christner

Lord Make Me Just a Drop of Oil

Not the Whole Can

TWILA CHRISTNER

WestBow
P R E S S
A DIVISION OF THOMAS NELSON

ISBN: 978-1-4497-4078-8 (e)
ISBN: 978-1-4497-4079-5 (sc)
ISBN: 978-1-4497-4080-1 (hc)

Library of Congress Control Number: 2012903630

WestBow Press books may be ordered through booksellers or by contacting:

WestBow Press
A Division of Thomas Nelson
1663 Liberty Drive
Bloomington, IN 47403
www.westbowpress.com
1-(866) 928-1240

Printed in the United States of America

WestBow Press rev. date: 3/21/2012

Chapter One

An Impression All Right ...
but Not the One I Wanted

Martha

Martha and I hadn't seen each other in twenty-five years. She remembered me as the goofball in school who made others laugh during class. I remembered her as a perfect girl, but one who had a low threshold for laughter. I would entertain those around me with various objects hidden just below the table, where the teacher couldn't see. Hey, I was bored. It really wasn't that funny. They must have been bored also. And for some reason—which I will leave to your imagination—my friends were always getting into trouble for laughing. They never reported me as the culprit, though. Perhaps they were too ashamed to admit that what they had laughed at was so trivial.

After twenty-five years, a person should forget things, right? Martha didn't. She called to tell me she and her husband were coming to see us. She recalled the two little plastic dogs I'd carried in my pencil case and the antics they would perform. My youthful pranks still lived on in her memory! But as I prepared for this visit, I was determined to show her that I had grown up, had children, and become a very mature person.

During our time together, we visited a nearby area that had a lot of Amish shops. One stop was at an older home that had been made into a fabric and novelty store. My daughter, Heather, and Martha went on ahead of me and were in the downstairs part when I came in. Because the Amish do not use electricity, the stairs were pretty dark. It didn't help any that there was a very dark, heavy set of curtains at the bottom that were designed to keep some of the heat downstairs. In this darkness, I did not see the yellow tape on one of the steps, marking it as shallower than the rest. I missed that step and went flying through the air. There was no railing, and as I flailed in every direction to grab hold of something, the drapes were my only salvation. But they only served as a rope to swing me right out into the room like a monkey. As if that weren't enough, I landed on a table piled with bolts of fabric. On impact, the bolts flew off the table, and I sat there, stunned. Worse yet, Martha and Heather were right there, facing my direction, and saw the whole thing.

Now, my daughter has grown up with my antics and is often embarrassed by these things. She often says, "Hey, that's my mom. She does things like that!" Martha, on the other hand, was immediately out of control with laughter and found the quickest way out of the store.

Heather helped me gather up the bolts of fabric and put them back. As for the curtains, there was little I could do to remedy that. Although the rod had not broken, it was in a sharp V shape with the curtains cowering in the middle.

We made a small purchase from the young Amish clerk, who couldn't seem to take her enlarged eyes off of me. When Heather and I got back to the van, we found Martha still sobbing with laughter. Our men, who had been waiting in the van, implored us to give them a speedy explanation as to what had happened. I lamely said, "Well, I fell, and Martha thinks it's funny." This remark sent Martha into more gales of laughter. My husband said that Martha had come out and crossed the street weeping so hard that she could hardly walk or talk.

As they tried to pump her for information, asking, "Where's Twila and Heather?" she only sobbed more and couldn't answer. Seeing her crying so hard, they began to worry that we had come to some serious harm.

Only as they started to get out of the van did my husband think to ask, "Are they all right?"

She managed to squeak out, "They're okay," and went on sobbing.

It wasn't until sometime later I got the vision of how that had to look in Martha's and the Amish girl's eyes. *Everything is peaceful and quiet. Suddenly, this woman—a size eighteen isn't really that small—comes swinging in on a curtain and lands on a table of fabric bolts.* Yes, had that been someone else, I'd have been laughing too. So much for proving I was no longer that high school class clown! This made those antics seem dull. Being an artist, I drew up a cartoon of the act and sent it to Martha some months later. She has kept it in her Bible all these years and told me anytime she needs a lift, she takes it out, looks at it, and weeps with laughter all over again. At my expense, I guess she gets a drop of oil now and then that keeps her machinery running smoothly.

Have you ever had times when just a little laughter has helped to lighten your load? One such time occurred when our daughter was in college. She had come home one weekend totally devastated. Some unfortunate circumstances had arisen, and a few people she had trusted had proven not to be true friends. She lay across my bed that evening, telling me all about it. I reached over, took a book off the nightstand, and said, "Heather, Lois loaned me this book, saying it might help at times like this. She says it's really funny!"

Heather responded, "Nothing, and I mean nothing, could make me laugh tonight."

I said, "Oh well, I'll read some of it anyway," and I commenced reading aloud. I don't remember the title or the author, but that dear lady had some of the funniest things happen to her. She had taken the trouble to put them into print, and now we were relating to some of them. I read on, and we were soon slapping the bed and laughing until the tears ran.

No, the book didn't change the situation any. It didn't fix any problems, but it did help to lift our spirits. At the time, I said, "Perhaps that's why so many unusual things have happened to me. I can tell them to others, and as they laugh at my experiences, it will be a drop of oil in their emotional machinery."

All right, Lord, I accept who You have made me to be. Maybe that unusual, embarrassing episode will help someone under a load. Possibly, some dear lady can find a little humor in those events I clearly didn't plan. I do accept being a drop of oil for You, Lord. But must I really be the whole can?

Nice Job!

Why is it that when you are trying to impress people with how smart you are, you end up doing the dumbest things right in front of them—or worse yet, in this case, right under their feet?

I know I had spent at least half an hour explaining to a lady how I was capable of correcting a mistake in such a way that she would be pleased.

My husband and I had taken a reupholstering class and had become pretty good at it. We had starred as teacher's pets and therefore received extra help. She had sweetly conned us into finishing a job that she had started and hated. We soon hated it too! It was a large, oddly shaped sectional couch.

Our customer wanted this couch for Thanksgiving, as she was having out-of-town guests. My husband and I worked long hours getting it ready for her to pick up late Thanksgiving Eve. The couch frames were done in one building and the cushions at our home. The customer made two stops and merrily took the furniture home to put it together, ready for company. That's when the bomb dropped.

The wisdom of Mother's words—which you don't pay attention to until it's too late—"Never change horses in the middle of the stream" became apparent. Our teacher had cut the new foam for the cushions before she had given us the job. She had a totally different method than I did. I proceeded with my method. I did a very neat job, but the cushions were four inches off! Yeah, I should have measured, but you live and learn.

As you would expect, the customer called my teacher and had every right to be mad. The teacher and I both felt guilty. She offered to drive me out two days after Thanksgiving to see what we could do. How sweet of her! Somehow, it became my problem, and being the good girl that I am, I said yes and went with her to tame this lion.

On the way, my teacher filled me in with information about our customer. "A nice lady, but has a husband that is hard to get to know. Just can't get on his wavelength," she said. Since my teacher drove the local ambulance, she would often meet this guy in the emergency room where he worked. "You can just never get next to him," she went on to say. It seemed to bug her, and I'm not sure why she felt I needed to know all of this, but we surely laughed about it later.

I still don't know how I got roped into fixing this boo-boo! As I said earlier, I spent half an hour convincing the lady that I could take the cushions apart and use the extra fabric that had been reserved for a rocker to redo the cushions. Since the rocker was small, I could use the cushion fabric for that. She finally felt that I could deliver a good product, so we headed out the door to the car. We all started down a very steep hill, the customer in the lead, then my teacher, and then me, all of us carrying a load of cushions. I awkwardly gathered up my portion and took hold of my son's hand. He was about two years old and was bundled into a heavy coat and hat. Good thing! Just as I stepped to the brink of the hill, I severely turned my ankle. I threw the cushions up into the air and fell hard to the ground. I jerked my son down in the process. As if that weren't bad enough, I began rolling down the hill and couldn't stop. In those moments of rolling like a kid on a summer frolic, I tried every method I could think of to stop myself. We had to be a sight—cushions bouncing everywhere, a large woman, tumbling downhill, and a little boy rolling right after her!

Lord, is this part of being a drop of oil? I don't get it. This really isn't funny ... at least to me! This wasn't in my plan for convincing this lady I am intelligent. Why this, Lord?

I know I was blushing furiously, before I ever came to a stop right against the lady's legs. There I lay, stunned, looking up under her dress as my son bumped against me. I could just imagine her thoughts: *Really bright gal here. Throws my cushions on the ground and hopes to use the fabric. She's so stupid she sees a hill and has to see if she can roll down it. Then, as if that were not enough, she even has her son do the same exercise!*

I frantically prayed God would send a small earthquake so the ground would swallow me, but before I could get the prayer finished, the pain in my ankle took all my attention.

The lady's husband had been out chopping some wood and had seen the whole thing. He came running up and told me to put my arm around his neck. Yes, the one who was "hard to get next to"! He gently eased me onto the car seat and started rubbing my ankle. As he rubbed, he explained what he was doing and how this method worked for sprains. I was amazed at how soon the pain let up. I was on his "wavelength."

On the way back to town, my teacher and I relived the whole incident. There she stood with her jacket clearly stating "E and E Ambulance" but doing nothing! She was trying to get her jaw off her chest. After all, here was this man who was so difficult to "get next to" on his first meeting with me saying, "Put your arm around my neck!"

The story has a good ending, in that I did redo the cushions to the customer's satisfaction. Miraculously, I had no more trouble with my ankle, which would usually lay me up for a week. Best of all, God spared me the embarrassment of ever running across them again, since they soon moved to Florida. God is good! He may seem a little late at times, but He's good anyway!

Chapter Two

Lord, Why Did You Take Your Hand off My Mouth?

Moose

It has taken years for me to learn to count to five before expressing myself quickly and clearly. They usually say one should count to ten before speaking. Well, I feel accomplished to get to five. That gives the Lord time to see it coming and occasionally get His hand over my mouth. Honestly, there are times I've reverently thanked the Lord for reaching me in time. Other times—well, I guess I didn't even get to number one!

At our house, if someone identifies something incorrectly, someone else is sure to call out, "Moose!"—thanks to me.

I am such a sharing person, it often gets me into trouble. If I see a beautiful scene or unusual phenomenon, I will probably quickly say, "Look! Quick!"—or whatever else hits my brain.

Most of my family lives in Colorado, so when we visit, we try to take in some of the attractions of that beautiful area. One such time, several of us planned to take a steam train ride in the mountains. It was an all-day ride over a pass with absolutely stunning scenery. It was just too breathtaking to observe through the coach windows, so most of the passengers spent the entire day in the open cars. At the end of the day, we were taken back over the pass in buses to our cars.

It had been a wonderful day. Spending the whole day out in the pure mountain air had made everyone relaxed and sleepy. Everyone was pretty much content to find a comfortable spot and shut down for the bus ride back. Oh, that I had shut down also! But being from the East, I wanted to relish every moment—engrave those mountain scenes in my memory. I sat with my nose nearly pressed to the window so as not to miss a single thing. I didn't.

We had been to Rocky Mountain National Park earlier and had the privilege of seeing lots of deer, elk, and even a moose. And now, sure enough, I spotted a moose. I didn't want to be the only one enjoying such a great animal. We would be passing it very quickly, so I loudly called, "A moose! Everyone, look! A moose"" Oh, what a scramble! Everyone came to life, grabbing cameras and rushing to my side of the bus. It is a wonder that it didn't turn over.

Alas, as everyone had their cameras pointed at the black object, it lifted its head. You could almost see its expression, "You wanted *my* picture?" It was a mule!

The rest is a blur. I was wallowing in embarrassment so deeply, I don't even know how the people responded. I knew buses had large storage areas under them for luggage—but try as I might, I couldn't find the door to crawl in.

I don't know if he really said it then, but whenever my husband tells this story, he always claims that he said, "Hey, I only have her out on a leave. I'm taking her back tomorrow!"

Lord, I really was just trying to share Your beauty. Why couldn't it have been a moose? Why did the dumb thing have to lift its head? I know you could have made a moose out of that mule in a quick miracle. Perhaps someone is still laughing to this day about the moose that turned into a mule. Perhaps they think of it in a down time and laugh. I am still not laughing, but use me as a drop of oil, Lord. Right now, however, I think I could easily fit in a can of oil.

Giraffe!

My husband has forbidden me from publicly identifying any animals in the future. Not long ago, we went to a sportsman store. They had an awesome display of mounted African animals caught by many brave hunters. The taxidermist had displayed the animals so well that you felt you were right there in the wild with them. I must admit I spent most of my time right there. Who cares about all the different fishing lures there are to be seen? To me, they are all the same—more to lure the fisherman than the fish. And rods and reels- again, to me, they are all the same. After all, I once caught enough nice bluegill to cook, and that was with a stick, some string, and pork and beans on a safety pin. They also had guns. How boring!

But, back to my story - On the way home, while my husband

was probably thinking about such boring stuff, I was still picturing those scenes and admiring the artist who could have painted the background in such a way to make the animals look so real. So, you see, we were both in our separate worlds when we saw a dead animal along the side of the road. Now, I was driving, so I have a bit of an excuse—I didn't have a chance to really observe what it was. That being said, I wished I had waited, at least a few seconds, before giving my verdict as to what the poor unfortunate creature was. I saw it had spots (like really big ones), was tan, and had rather long legs, so when my husband wonderingly said, "What was that?" I quickly responded, "A giraffe!"

The second it was out, I desperately started grabbing for every feasible reason as to why a giraffe would be lying dead along the side of the road in the middle of Ohio. Could have been a baby one had fallen from a circus truck, or perhaps it was someone's pet that had gotten loose. Instantly, my husband was slapping the dash and choking with laughter. Our daughter, in the backseat, was no better. When she and he could finally catch their breaths and had wiped away their tears, they started making comments like, "Yeah, here in Ohio we have signs up, 'Look out for giraffe crossings.'" This was followed by more laughter! "These giraffes have really short necks, and the spots are only on their backs. These are more commonly known as baby deer. Better yet, fawns. A moose, and now a giraffe! Please just leave animal identification to someone else."

I really didn't appreciate all the humor of it until I lay awake that night and thought of how ridiculous that would be. I nearly woke my husband shaking with laughter.

Recently, we were riding along a country road at dusk, and I saw a deer. Now, for a few minutes, it looked unmistakably like a deer. I think that I have moved up on the ladder of intelligence by now. I actually waited long enough to see clearly that my "deer" was a mailbox.

I had almost chalked up another failing grade in animal identification. God kept his hand over my mouth on that one. Thank you, Jesus. Proverbs 17:28 says, "Even a fool, when he holdeth his peace, is counted wise: and he that shutteth his lips is esteemed a man of understanding." Believe me. I am getting wiser.

Wig the Pig

It was such a cute little baby pig, and I really didn't say that much. I thought my husband, Bill, was the only one who had heard me.

You see, I was raised on a farm about one hundred years ago— well, shave that down to about half—but I still melt when I see a baby farm animal.

As a small girl, I thought nothing was more fun than adopting a "runt" piglet whose mother had rejected it. Daddy would bring it into the house wrapped in his coat. We girls would wrap it in towels, put it in a cardboard box by the woodstove, and hand-feed it. Forget dolls! One such little guy we named Wig. He never lacked for all the love and attention a small animal could desire. He endured being dressed in doll clothes and taking rides in doll buggies and red wagons. He had the life! And he flourished well with that life. As we played in the yard, Wig followed us around like a puppy dog. Even our farm dog accepted him as one of us. Wig didn't have to stay within the electric fence like the rest of his brothers. As he got bigger, he even had a special bed in the chicken house.

Then the unthinkable happened. With so much love lavished on him, how could he ever be so ungrateful as to run away? He didn't go far, only a quarter of a mile to the neighbors' cane field. Cane is sweet, and eating cane to a pig is like eating candy is to a child. We girls could understand that, but we wanted him home at least at night. Being a pig, he found it comfortable enough just to lie down in the field. To me, it would be like eating candy all day and then lying down in a chocolate factory for the night, only to get up and eat candy all the next day. We felt he was being very ungrateful not to nestle down in the special bed that we had made for him. Our occasional sightings of him, however, showed it agreed with him. Every few days, one of us would spot him as he crossed the road to get a drink at the stream that crossed our pasture. Daddy tried every conceivable way to get him back, but he was a smart pig.

On Thanksgiving Day of that year, when the house was full of relatives, Daddy announced, "After we eat, we're going to have a Wild West roundup and catch Wig the Pig." Aunts, uncles, cousins, brothers, and sisters—everyone was going to help get this done. I was excited! We were going to get our pet back. I intended to lift his floppy ear and give him a lecture on thankfulness.

Daddy formed a plan and had all of us line up across the road where the pig always crossed. Daddy was to scare him out, and wherever the pig crossed, the closest person was to grab him and hold on until the others could come help. Good plan. Smart pig! Wouldn't you know, the frightened pig saw all the people, paused a bit, and then headed for the weakest spot—me! I made an all-out effort to grab him, but I had not grown as fast as my pig had. He was almost full grown. He made a dash toward me, ran between my legs, and spilled me on the gravel road. It was another failed attempt that sent everyone back to the house laughing.

When the weather began to turn really cold, Wig must have sensed he needed more shelter. Wig allowed the dog at the grain elevator to round him up and hurry him toward the office. Old Bill, the grain elevator's operator, saw the dog and pig coming and opened the office door. Sure enough, the pig and dog came right in. Bill called Daddy, who took his stock truck there and backed up to the door. Wig didn't even get unloaded at our home, as a neighbor had told Daddy that he wanted to buy him. That neighbor put Wig in a shed for the night, but Wig was found dead the next morning. Daddy said he was sure the pig had died of a broken heart when he found his days of freedom were over. Although that was only one of our "runts," we girls felt bad for him. Daddy comforted us with reassurance that we would have more pigs to nurture. I'm sure we did, but none ever had the impact on our lives that Wig did. Probably because of this, baby pigs always worm right into my heart.

Since my children were raised in the city, one day, I came up with the bright idea to take them to a livestock auction in a nearby town. It would be a good place for them to see horses, cows, pigs, and goats. My husband thought it was a good idea too. We were watching the different animals go through when a worker brought in a cute little baby pig. Nobody bid on him. I know I'm way too sentimental. I looked at Bill and said, "Honey, that's a pity. He needs a home." I know I didn't say it very loud.

The auctioneer stopped the sale right there and looked at me. He called out over the PA system, "Ma'am, if you'd like him—we'll just give him to you."

All eyes in the crowded sale barn were on me. My husband wanted to melt into the bench!

Another man yelled, "Hey, I'll give you a blanket to take him home in."

Another called out, "I'll give you some feed." By this time, I think everyone was ready to jump on the bandwagon to my embarrassment.

Now I was really torn! Here was a precious little pig's life hanging in the balance at my hands. How could I raise a pig (only to become a hog) in town on a small lot? If I didn't, he would probably be done away with. Another little Wig the Pig. All these people could clearly see I was all heart (perhaps no brain) and were offering their bits to my husband's utter embarrassment.

One look at my husband's eyes told me his answer. He always had such clear thinking and would not, even in a nightmare, have considered taking that pig. Finally, after enough tense moments, he said, "No, she won't be taking the pig." Many attendees intensified the drama with "awws" that slid down the musical scale.

After the auctioneer started again, my husband leaned over and said, "I can't even take you to a sale barn without your drawing attention to us!" He hates being in the spotlight but gets his share as he walks with me and I stumble into full view. Poor man!

I know the auctioneer got a kick out of it, because he brought it up again later when he saw us talking. "Hey," he called, "you can still have the pig. Have you changed your mind?"

Before long, my husband felt we needed to get the children home. I really think he was afraid I'd end up with a crippled horse or three-legged goat. Well, at least my heart is in the right place! I just read on Facebook the other day something that goes like this: "When we die, we will not be remembered so much for what we did, but more for how we loved." You see, I'm working on that one! Perhaps my head isn't always in the right place, but, even though it sometimes gets me in trouble, I do hope I have love.

Chapter Three

Not Me! I Didn't Do That!

Rejected Roses

One day, someone was pounding on the front door and I hurried to see who it was. There stood a guy carrying a box with a dozen red, long-stem roses. I must have shown my surprise, as he sweetly said, "Some guy has sent you flowers." Thinking rapidly is a good thing most of the time, but it often gets me into trouble. I was furious! I only had one guy in my life, and that was my husband! Whom could this guy be who was trying to make a good impression on me? I didn't get the man's name, because I so adamantly made it clear that no man was sending me roses. The delivery boy said, "Oh, excuse me, maybe I have the wrong address," and left.

I went storming out the back door to where my husband was working on a flower bed.

"Just think of it!" I fairly shouted. "Some guy is trying to impress me and send flowers! A guy was just at the front door with flowers from some man I don't even know, but I sent him packing! I'm not taking flowers from any guy—you are the only man in my life! The audacity"!

The look of shock on my husband's face fired me up even more. I was talking so fast, he could not even get a word in edgewise. If nothing else came out of it, my husband was surely getting an idea of my loyalty to him!

Finally, putting his hand out to slow my monologue, he asked, "Where is he?"

I pointed down the alley, where the poor man was slinking off like a dog with his tail between his legs. To my shock, my husband started running after him. Now I was the one worried, being sure my husband was going to beat him to a pulp for delivering flowers to his wife. I hoped he would be rather easy on him; after all, he was only the delivery boy, not the man who had sent the flowers.

I peeked around the edge of the house to see my husband take the box of roses from the man and start walking back toward me. When he got back, he held out the roses and said, "Twila, I can't even try to surprise you without you messing it up! It is your birthday today! Happy birthday dear."

Again, I had to thank the Lord for giving me a husband with an overload of patience. Bill has had so many occasions to look up a divorce lawyer, but so far, he has left the telephone book sitting on the shelf.

In or Out!

Back when I was a girl, if a fire truck came screaming by your house, it was just understood that you dropped everything to rush and see what happened. My brother's friend was at our house one day when this happened. He and my brother jumped into his truck to go see what was going on. I was overseeing a group of children, and of course, they wanted to see, too. I, being the oldest, saw that each child was carefully stowed into the back of the pickup truck (another modern-day no-no) and then slammed the tailgate and climbed up on the bumper to get in myself. Well, when the driver heard the tailgate slam, he assumed that everyone was in and, without looking around, took off. I had just placed both feet on the bumper and had a good grip on the tailgate when away we went. The takeoff was so fast, I could not even think of climbing into the truck bed. There I clung to the tailgate for dear life. Finally, my brother looked around and said, "Hey, one didn't get in!" The driver took a quick look and slammed on the brakes so hard I knew I would fall hard into the bed of the truck if I tried to move. Not wanting to hurt my pride, I braced until he had slowed enough that I could get over the tailgate with dignity. He gave me what he thought was plenty of time to do it and without looking, took off again. This happened three times. First, I was leaning out the back, hanging on so as not to fall on the pavement, and then I was bracing, trying not to fall hard into the bed in a disgraceful manner.

In my mind's eye, I could see the whole college group gathered at the fire down the road when this truck would arrive—the back full of children and a "dignified" college girl, dress flapping above her knees, hair flying in the wind, hanging onto the tailgate as though she were a fireman. I did not relish the scene. I did not want to arrive on the scene of the fire in such a manner that even the firemen might forget where the water was supposed to go. I could visualize their diverted attention when they saw a girl so desperate to get to the fire that she would hang onto the back of a truck. That place was for firemen not college girls in dresses. That scene was not going to happen!

Mercifully, my brother looked again. Again, he told the driver of the dilemma. The driver must have been disgusted. One more time, he furiously slammed the brakes. By this time, I was already half dead with embarrassment and was in danger of falling off and getting killed. I had made up my mind if I got another chance, I'd do something desperate to change the scene. This time, I was going to fall into the truck with my loving family and friends. As he slowed for the last time, I let go and splattered into the back of the truck.

Later in life, I saw this scenario repeated when I gave my heart to Jesus. I wanted to come to Him so pure and right, everything intact, and perfect. What He wanted was for me to come just as I was. I had put it off, thinking I would improve myself—become a better person (daintily step over that tailgate). I would walk in all intact, every sin taken care of, already a perfect girl. No, His desire was for me to fall at His feet, letting Him pick me up. Finally, one day, inwardly, I just threw up my hands and said, "Lord, here I come! This isn't very pretty, but I want to be safe with You." I quit the rocking, almost in, almost out, and made the plunge. It was a happy morning when I fell at His feet at the cross and into the love and safety of God. It's great to get off the tailgate and get in.

Sticking my Neck Out

There have been too many times in my life when I wish that I could point to the one next to me and say, "It wasn't me! She did it!" Unfortunately, I am usually the one who has to step up to the plate and say, "It was me. I didn't plan it. I didn't premeditate it. It just happened!" The laughter, then, is all directed toward me.

While we were in college, one of my girlfriends talked me into going out to the airport in Colorado Springs to see the president of the United States arrive. We went to our jobs early that day and worked hard to be able to get off in time to do this. Already having spent our energies, we rushed to the airport a whole three hours ahead of time. We wanted to get a place in front so we would have a good view. With no place to sit down, hot pavement, and a crowd of people behind us, it just wasn't the most pleasant place to be. But we were going to see the president, do or die. Perhaps we would even get to shake hands with him; what else mattered? As time dragged on, the people kept pushing from behind, squeezing me against the rope. I began to wonder why I had been so pushy to be first in line! Men in uniform soon sized up the situation and began ordering the people to stop pushing and back off a little.

Then, he arrived! The pushing began in earnest. But I got to shake hands with him! My goal! Then I realized I wanted a picture of this occasion, so I leaned out over the rope as far as I could with camera in hand. I got my picture all right, but in my excitement, I did not see the marine guard standing so close. I got my hair hopelessly tangled in the decorations on his coat. There I was with my head stuck to the shoulder of this man in his dress uniform. *Embarrassing* is an understatement in describing my dilemma. He never made a move (what training!) as I jerked and messed with my hair trying to get it free. There was no escaping to disappear into the crowd; they had me pinned. There were no manholes in the pavement and moving forward would've only gotten me shot. I stood there and turned all shades of red, wishing I were the same race as he so my embarrassment would not make me stand out like Rudolph's nose. For another half hour, I had to stand within a foot of that man, as he looked steadfastly forward, as though nothing had happened. That was embarrassing enough, but the local newspaper caught my image, which appeared on the front page of the daily paper. Talk about sticking your neck out! It's been some thirty years, but I still blush when I look at that newspaper clipping. Why me? I'm about ready to believe that God allows some things to happen to keep us humble. Truthfully, I was not proud, only excited and happy. But in the end, I was also very embarrassed. Are you molding me, Lord, or is this another drop of oil?

The Peanut Butter Jar

It's dreadful to be fourteen hundred miles away from your mother, especially when you need to talk to her about something really private. I was married back in the dark ages, so I didn't know a lot about some things. I'd been to a doctor when I broke my finger in high school, but other than that, I was green as a gourd about going to a doctor. Healthy girl that I was, I had very little experience concerning doctors. Mother could have filled me in, but money was tight, so we didn't call much and only communicated by snail mail.

We'd been married nearly a year when I suspected that I was pregnant. I called and set up an appointment with a doctor. I was told to collect a sample—the first—after rising on the day of the appointment. I didn't consult anyone but was concerned about that "first." This troubled me; if they wanted the "first," how was I going to know when the first was over? How did you shut off the middle or the last? I decided to take it all, and they could judge what was first, middle, or last. I had no idea how much it would be, so I got an empty three-pound peanut butter jar, washed it up, and was ready. Catching it all, I knew that evasive "first" would be somewhere in there and they could find it. I ended up being correct. They found it.

We only had one car at the time, and my husband worked twenty minutes away. He would get home at three fifty, and my appointment was at four. I'd just have time to cross town and arrive on time. I had no idea one could spend hours waiting on a doctor and that I wouldn't have gotten a pink slip for being a minute late. But late I would not be.

As soon as I saw my husband arrive, I tore down the apartment steps with my treasured "sample"—more like the whole barrel—in a brown paper bag. I jumped into the car and sped away. As I went around a corner, my bag rolled off the seat and onto the floor. To my horror, I saw my jar was not liquid proof. I stopped at a traffic light and righted my jar, hoping my "first" had not gotten away. When I got to the office, I realized my soggy bag wasn't fit to carry my jar in. Instant panic! What was I going to do? After a quick prayer, I opened the trunk, and to my joy, someone had left a very large brown paper grocery bag there. Boy! was God ever on my side! That bag would have held twenty dollars' worth of groceries back then. More important, it would hold my jar so no one would see how much my "first" was. Regaining my composure, I carried my bag in, set it beside my chair, and waited forever with the other patients. When I was called in, I didn't think anything about it when the nurse asked for my sample and took a double look. After all, one needed to look twice to take it all in.

Later, I was sweetly congratulated that I was going to have a baby and all that goes with that. But I thought the nurse just might be trying to insult me when she handed me a teensy-weensy little bottle and said, "This is for your next sample." Then I was the shocked one. How would the "first" ever fit in that? Much less, how would I ever hit it? I know now that those nurses have been laughing and talking all these thirty-three years about the lady with the huge sample. I suppose that has been a drop of oil in a nurse's hectic life. I'm sure they could write a book about such things; I just added another chapter.

"Lord, I will be a drop of oil for you, but please, just delete my name."

Stuck!

I appreciate the fact that God answers our quick little prayers. Someone said if God did everything we asked Him to do, He would be serving us, instead of us serving Him—sort of like a genie in a jar. We would just clap our hands, and presto, everything would be happily ever after. I would like to have done that the time our car died in the middle of an intersection, in deep water. People in their cars were honking at me, but I could do nothing about it, as my car was flooded.

I am thankful I had a cell phone and was able to call AAA. I prayed they would hurry, and they did. When the tow truck came, my daughter and I had to get out of the car. There we were, stomping in water up over our ankles. The driver told us to get into the truck. My daughter climbed in, and I tried to. My arthritis was not so bad then, but bad enough that I could not manage to get in on my own.

With people in cars sitting all around watching, my daughter bailed back out to help me. I know I probably looked like a duffel bag, but I didn't have those convenient handles a duffel bag had to move it about. I'm sure paramedics wish people had them, and I surely could have used a good set right then.

We splashed around with our long dresses swishing in the water while we tried to find a proper way to boost me up onto the running board. The only leverage she could get was to put her hands under my bahoomba and shove. I'm sure we made a three-ring circus getting into that truck, complete with audience.

You see, if God were my servant, I would have asked Him to make the car start so that I could drive away without a scene. But I am His servant and thanked Him for the help He sent. Perhaps one of God's children was in one of those cars watching and needed a little laughter. Perhaps God used me to accomplish it.

I'd like to think that people in those vehicles would never see me again or remember. I don't suppose I could be that lucky, as we live in a rather small community. Of course, my imagination tells me that probably every once in a while someone sees me and points me out to his or her friends, saying, "Look, there is that lady! She is the one who was stomping around in deep water, trying to get into a tow truck! Finally, after we had waited for ages, a girl pushed her up into the truck." Then lots of laughter follows yet, another drop of oil…

Chapter Four

Remodeling Is for the Lionhearted

The Mole

The average woman reacts when she sees a mouse scurrying across her kitchen floor—some definitely more than others. I would come in the class of "more." On this occasion, however, I surprised even myself at how calmly I reacted. We came home one night to see a small, dark body rush for cover under a cupboard. I noticed that it was somewhat larger than your ordinary mouse and didn't hurry as fast as a mouse usually does. My husband said, "Oh, it's a mole."

But nonetheless, moles and human beings were not designed to abide in the same dwelling. He had to go! The only reason this creature had even considered entering was because we were in the process of remodeling our home and there were lots of gaps in the walls where reconstruction was taking place. The cooler weather encouraged him to try his luck at cohabitating with us. Wrong move! I was pleased I had not screamed, because I can never see a mouse without giving it hearing problems.

"Honey, just go over there and scare it out. When it comes this way," this brave mother said (after all, it seemed so slow compared to a mouse), "I'll throw your work boot on it, stop it, and then you can take it outside." Good plan!

Just like he knew our schedule, it ran straight for me. I had the boot raised and ready to strike, but as he neared, I did the thing that comes most naturally to me—I gave a bloodcurdling scream and jumped up on a chair. It's a wonder the mole didn't die of heart failure. Instead, he altered his course and headed for our bedroom, of all places. That room was a mess because it was one of the rooms that was most under construction. We hunted high and low and never did find him. We believe to this day, I scared it right back outside through the hole it had come in. I know he held his little paw to his heart in a prayer of thankfulness to God that he had escaped a maniac woman.

We soon settled down and got ready for bed. My husband asked if he could have a bowl of ice cream. Ironically, that day, I had cleaned out a drawer and found a little gray rubber mouse. My husband is the king of "never being startled," so I had thought it would be fun to put it on his pillow. For once, maybe I could rattle his cage a little. No effect! While I was in the kitchen getting the ice cream, he had pulled back the spread, found the mouse, and slipped it under a stack of folded clean sheets I had put on the end of the bed. I came back, moved the sheets, and found the mouse. Again, I was so proud I had not screamed. I know my weakness, so I decided to hold the mouse in my hand until I finished my bowl of ice cream. Come tomorrow, I'd find a place for that mouse, but for now, I'd keep it right there in my hand where it couldn't scare me anymore.

As we talked, Bill finished his ice cream and lay down. I sat and talked with him—all the time subconsciously disturbed about not having found that mole. Distracted by our conversation, I suddenly thought, *What am I holding so tight in my hand?* So I opened my hand, and before I could stop myself, I screamed and threw the mouse and my bowl in the air. The bowl of ice cream landed upside down on my husband's stomach. Thankfully, he has a good sense of humor and puts up with my idiosyncrasies. Most men would have looked up a divorce lawyer the next day. I found that mouse the other day and was startled—but it ain't gonna happen again. I threw it out! I made sure it was in the bottom of the wastebasket so no one would find it and give it the life it was probably designed for in the first place—to scare someone.

I do believe it was only by the grace of God I got through those years of remodeling, along with raising children in the mess.

The New Shirt

I could write a book on remodeling. One really should move clear out of the house while it is going on. Even a motel with no kitchen would make living easier. But we were afforded no such luxury, so for about the space of five years, one room after another would be in complete chaos. The kitchen was the worst with the bath being second. It was my job to get meals for friends who came each evening to do the work. My husband would trade his labor in helping them remodel their homes, thus keeping the cost of labor down. It worked well for all of us financially but certainly took a long time.

One night, when the kitchen was all torn up, I was trying to clean up from the evening meal, while my father was putting in a new kitchen sink. There were at least three other men there helping. My brother-in-law, who really wasn't helping much—I think he had just come to see the circus—was standing around watching. Now I was seven months pregnant with our daughter and a bit clumsy. I did my best to navigate the obstacle course, which was constantly changing. Somehow that night, I managed to stumble over a board and was headed for the floor. As was my usual custom, I gave my unnerving scream on the way down and grabbed for anything—just anything—to save me. It so happened that my brother-in-law was the closest object, and my hands found his nice new shirt. I did save my fall—but stripped away every button off that new shirt. Of course, I didn't see his reaction because I was busy saving myself.

My mother, who was sitting and watching, got a ringside view of the whole thing. She laughed until she nearly had a heart attack. She told me later she woke up in the night and laughed some more. She still gets tickled when she thinks about it. She said the abject horror on his face was first, followed by a desperate grab to close his shirt, and then anger. I'm not sure what made him mad—my scream or the stripping of his new shirt of all its buttons. Hey, he saved my fall and possibly the life of his dear little niece with whom he fell in love a couple months later. He should have been happy to sacrifice a shirt's buttons for her, shouldn't he?

The guys told us when we gutted our bathroom, "It will only be messed up one day." Wrong! The morning of the second day found me in too much of a hurry to make it to the neighbor's house to use the bathroom. I grabbed a five-gallon bucket and tried to keep it secret from my husband, but have you ever poured water quietly into an empty five-gallon bucket at five thirty in the morning? No, I can still see my husband's face as he appeared around the corner to see what was going on. I think the sound got to him, because he was going to wait until he got to work, but I soon heard the same sound. I told him, "They say, years later, you'll laugh over some of this." He didn't exactly see the humor that morning or several days later either as the project dragged out. We had the key to the neighbor's house to use her facilities, and thankfully, she was half blind and deaf, so we didn't bother her as we made endless trips in and out.

People recall "the good old days" and relish pictures of old outhouses—they can have it! No good old days for me! I had enough of that on the farm growing up. That gave me a refresher course on appreciation for indoor plumbing. We are to thank the Lord for the small things, but I see indoor plumbing as a very large thing to thank the Lord for. I am also thankful that the remodeling is over.

The Bat!

We probably had more crazy things happen while we were remodeling than anyone else on earth. Trying to exist in the chaos and take care of two little children at the same time was very exhausting. One night, when our daughter was just a baby, I was especially worn to a frazzle. I was so tired, and she just would not go to sleep. Finally, after rocking and singing to her a lot, I was able to put her in her crib. As I crawled into bed with the lights out, I felt something swoosh across my face. I was so tired. I was not sure what was going on. I said to my husband, "Billy, something's wrong. I think I'm losing my mind!"

He said, "What's wrong?"

I replied, "I don't know; something brushed across my face."

He reached over and turned on the light. Just then, we saw what the problem was. A bat had gotten in one of the openings as we were replacing the windows. It was dive-bombing back and forth across the room. That was what I had felt brush across my face. I didn't scream, so my daughter slept on. I ran for the broom, gave it to my husband, and told him to use it. Like a pro baseball player, he swung as the bat came toward him. He did a crack shot, and it fell down over behind my rocking chair. There it was making eerie, squeaky noises. Brave mother that I am, I ran for the dustpan and told him scoop it up and take it outside. He did, and we settled down again.

I had just dozed off when I heard a strange beeping sound—a high-pitched beep followed by lower-pitched beeps. Again, I thought I had had too much and woke Billy. He got up again to see what the problem was. He looked all around and finally decided it must be the bat that he had thrown outside. He went outside to look. I thought if he was brave enough to go outside to look, I'd be brave and look inside. I found the problem. While batting at the bat, we had knocked the receiver of the telephone off the hook. I replaced it and called Billy back in. He said that the bat had flown away. Again, we settled down to try to sleep.

It seemed I had barely gotten to sleep when someone was pounding on the back door. Again, we bailed out of bed to find Billy's brother had come to pick him up, as it was time for him to go to work. We scrambled to get ready in as short a time as possible, and they rushed off to work. Would this craziness ever stop? I sank into my rocking chair, got my Bible, read, and prayed. I asked the Lord to help me get through this remodeling time. I have vowed I will never again live in a house while it is being remodeled. Such unthinkable things kept happening. Some people say the Lord takes you into the workshop and uses sandpaper to sand down your rough edges. I thought all my rough edges were gone. This remodeling was taking care of every sharp edge I ever had. By this time, I was feeling I was as smooth as a ping-pong ball. May He just keep me bouncing where He wants me in the game of life.

Chapter Five

My Hair-Trigger Scream!

Used for Good

I hate it that I scream so easily over absolutely nothing! I'd like to think that by this time in life, I'd have reached a measure of maturity, but a scream over a relatively small incident makes everyone within a block question that fact. It's not always bad. Once, my daughter and I actually averted an accident by screaming! We were coming around a corner near our home when a man pulled out of a gas station just as we arrived. Both my daughter and I saw that we were going to broadside him even though she was standing on the brakes and maneuvering as best she could. Instinctively, we both screamed at the same time. Now, our windows were up and so were the windows of the car we were about to hit. We screamed so loudly he actually heard us. He spun his head around, saw us about to impact him, and stomped on his gas pedal. We probably missed him by an inch. I can still see his large eyes as he spun and faced us in those seconds.

You should have seen the people pumping gas. They too heard the screams, but by the time they looked, the emergency was over. They are probably still wondering where the sound came from.

Another time, although I didn't plan it, my scream was used for good. I was sitting in my van waiting for my friends as they took their baby in to see the doctor. I was reading and looked up to see a young lady carrying her small child toward the office door. The sidewalk had a slope in it that was marked with yellow paint. Apparently, the mother didn't see the slope and lost her balance. She started to fall, and before I could help it, I screamed dreadfully as she was on her way down. She threw the child and landed hard, but they weren't hurt. The second she landed, I saw her frantically look around to see who had screamed. Those in the office did too. They came rushing out to help, but no one was hurt. I quickly rolled up my window and tried to appear busy reading. The next time I took my friends to that doctor there was a fence in place so no one would have that accident again. I may be crippled, but perhaps God used me to build a fence! He is good like that!

The Tigers!

I did it again. My wonderful image of "model motherhood" lay in gold-edged, shattered pieces at my feet. I had reached for the invisible stars that pretty fall afternoon and then gave a bloodcurdling scream that froze everyone in their tracks. What a mother!

It was my children's school trip to a farm where a lady kept wild animals that she had rescued. Her entire yard was filled with cages of exotic and some not-so-exotic animals that had been ill or abandoned that she had nursed back to health. Thus, she had her own personal zoo and enjoyed having groups come to see them. She would have let the children in to see the monkey that was dangling around in a sort of greenhouse, but the day was cool, and she was afraid he might catch a cold if she opened the door to let us in. Personally, I was glad. My children didn't need to be petting any old stinky monkey! It was fine for the animals to be behind bars and fences, but she took the children right over to a lion cub and allowed them to pet it. Now, come on, this "baby" stood as tall as the tallest boy among them when it put its front feet over the top of the pen. I was sweating as my son scratched the creature's ears and petted it as though it were his kitten at home. After all, I have read millions of stories of how these seemingly harmless animals one day turn vicious, smell a drop of blood, and attack without warning.

But my greatest fear came when she went to show us her prized possessions—two Bengal tigers, which she had raised along with her own children. She was telling how the one would shoot down the slide into the swimming pool with her daughter. The other she would take out in parades and all would be well, as long as the band didn't play so loudly that the tiger couldn't hear her voice.

As she explained the power of these animals, she opened the first cage surrounding one of the tigers and let the group into the first outer cage. I could not possibly imagine that she would open the inner cage and allow the children to pet these animals also. She seemed so sure of her animals, and I figured I was the only one with any doubts. She told us that the strength of their tails could break a leg.

Good mother that I am, I begin to plan an escape route should she decide to open that pen. If something went wrong. *Let's see, I'll grab Heather [my daughter] and Alan [my son] by the arms, rush back through this gate, and slam it shut.* Sorry about the luck of those poor other souls who would be locked inside ready to become the next "Happy Meal" for the tiger!

Neat plan! So, I slowly slid to the back of the group with my children until I was positioned right at the open gate. I made certain no one was behind me to hinder my rapid escape route and began my vigilant guard of the cage lock. Just as I was beginning to feel secure in my ability to overcome this great danger, something grabbed my backside. Already tense because my children's lives were at stake, I gave it all I had. It was probably one of the loudest screams I had done in a long time.

Abject terror covered everyone's face for a moment, and then I saw the looks on their faces. It was as if they wanted to find an escape route from me. Which should they choose? Take their chances with the tigers or be left to the tender mercies of a madwoman? I registered all this in the seconds it took to shut off my scream. I swung around to face my adversary: a naughty, trembling goat, who had innocently thought the flowers on my skirt might taste sweet. It didn't take him long to find another pasture.

Needless to say, our host did not open the cage. Whether she planned on doing so or not, I will never know. I know the others thought I needed to be admitted to a home for the bewildered. What a mother!

How often I have found myself in a similar situation spiritually. I start to think about how fierce and powerful the devil is, and trembling with fear over what he might do, I scramble about making plans to protect myself and my children. Some circumstances seem to creep up from behind and grab us and leave us paralyzed with fear. Sure that the devil has me now, I scream in fear but turn to find it is only the gentle tug of the Holy Spirit reminding me that "not by (my) might, nor by (my) power, but by His Spirit" (Zechariah 4:6) will I have the strength that I need to overcome the devil. I must not let the little "goats" eat away my joy—or get my goat.

The Mailman Changes Routes

For years, we had the friendliest mailman. He was a delight, and the children loved him. He always had something cheerful to say and kidded with the children as he kept walking. One day, I heard him laughing uproariously and looked out the window to see my son down on his stomach in a mud puddle flailing his arms and legs. The mailman had told him to swim. Alan was covered from head to toe in mud. The mailman thought it was hilariously funny.

One day, however, one of his jokes backfired on him. I had come home from the library with the children and was getting out of the car. Our mailbox was on the back side of the house right beside where we parked the car. The children had gotten out and saw the mailman coming, but I didn't. I was trying to get out with two five-pound bags of sugar and twenty-five library books. I was half in and half out when the mailman, who had just come around the corner, snorted on purpose.

When he snorted, I slung the books at his feet and threw the sugar. That surprised him enough, but my scream just made him wilt. He helped me gather up the books and the (thankfully) still-intact bags of sugar. Although he apologized, I think he secretly enjoyed it because he tried it several more times. He got used to my reactions.

He retired, and they gave us a new mailman. He was a young guy and of a totally different disposition. Although he never planned to scare me, it happened anyway. One day, I had come home from the store and was bothered because I couldn't find my coin purse. I went back out to the car and with the driver's door open was digging around to see if I could find it. I was thinking burglar—someone had stolen it from me— when I turned around and saw a man two feet away from me. Instinctively, I screamed. My daughter was standing there and had seen the mailman coming. She said she had tried to tell me the mailman was coming, but I had my mind on the coin purse and didn't hear her. Obviously, he was not used to such reactions. He shook all over and stuttered as he tried to get the words out. Heather says to this day, she has never seen a grown man so scared.

This new mailman would put the mail in the box by our back door and then take a shortcut across our lawn to the neighbors'. Our old mailman would never do that. The new one soon didn't either. One bitter winter day, I went out to our shed to get something. I was backing out the door with an armful when I glanced over my shoulder to see a man with a ski mask over his face coming right at me. Before I realized it was the mailman, I had again paralyzed him with my scream. I really did feel sorry for him. His eyes got as big as the holes in his mask.

Sometime later, on a Saturday, when my husband was home, he saw this guy carefully peeking around the side of the house and then dashing to the mailbox and hurrying away. He was truly scared. It wasn't long before we had a new mailman again. I saw this young guy delivering mail to the businesses uptown. I'm afraid he asked to change routes. He just couldn't handle ours.

I hate it when I realize I have made life difficult for someone, even though I had no intention of doing so. What one mailman enjoyed, the other found totally unbearable. I'm afraid instead of oil in his machinery, I was putting in sand.

Chapter Six

Mother's Orders: "Be Quiet in Church!"

The Light Bulb

I do not consider myself a nervous person. There have been times, when under extreme pressure, I have even surprised myself. But when things happen suddenly, I can't be sure what I might do. One Sunday morning, a nice young man was explaining scripture when a bulb in one of the hanging light fixtures burst. Somehow, water had leaked into it, and at that quiet moment, it did the strangest thing. There was a loud pop, and then, almost as if in slow motion, the bulb drifted to the floor and smashed. Leave it to me. Before the bulb ever reached the floor, I gave an awful scream—not only that, my feet flew up so high, I kicked the bench ahead of me. That scared everyone and made other ladies let out exclamations. For a few minutes, it was chaos—not because of danger, though. The bulb was up in a corner at the front, and no one was near it.

My poor dear husband said later, "We would all have been fine if you hadn't screamed." The speaker looked over the situation, turned it over to the hands of the custodian, and tried to proceed. But every once in a while, the scene I had caused would surface in his mind, and he would lose control and laugh again. I wanted to crawl under the bench, but that would only have added to their mirth.

My husband was spared one such event. I had gone with our children to a church camp in the fall. It was slightly cool, so the custodian had stoked the woodstove in the meeting hall. He had gone a little overboard, and it was so very hot inside. Those near the windows and doors had opened them a little so at least we could breathe. This building was right in the center of a hickory grove, and a lot of woodland creatures seemed interested in entering those open doors to draw near the fire. Unfortunately, I was seated on the aisle near the door. I was a bit entertained with the large bugs, spiders, and woolly worms crawling past me headed for the front. One large guy sitting further up decided certain bugs might be harmful and extended a large foot out into the aisle to exterminate them.

My daughter was sitting at a right angle to me where we could clearly see each other. She would smile when she saw him smashing those creatures. Once, she caught my eye and mouthed to me, "Mama, don't scream!" Me scream? Why would I? Of course not. She mouthed further, "There's a spider on you."

My mind works really fast at times like these. I was thinking, *Spider, cute little thing crawling on my skirt.* But to my horror, when I looked down, crawling up my bust and only a few inches from my eyes was a very large spider. Now I know he was probably harmless, but in that second, seeing those long legs reaching for the next step sent me out of control. Don't scream? Heather knew me too well. Scream I did, as I made a frantic swipe to remove him. That was the end of the meeting. The speaker was giving a rather serious talk, but everyone, the speaker included, burst into laughter, and we were dismissed. I hurried out into the dark to my cabin. I was doing anything but laughing. Why do I do these things?

I have to wonder why God would allow me to do the things I do. I know I am His child, so why would He allow me to disrupt a service? Did He see someone was under a load and that a little laughter would help to lift it? Had we sat long enough and needed to go to bed? Did He feel someone was going to take that speech a little too seriously and be depressed? I don't understand, but I know that God loves me, and I constantly ask Him to keep His arm around my shoulders and His hand over my mouth. I am desirous to be a tool in God's hands and really do try to walk carefully with my hand in His. Sometimes, I wonder if He must be using me like a toy photographers suddenly produce at a photo shoot to make a child laugh. Think how that toy might feel—grabbed out of a box, held up, perhaps squeezed to make a squawking sound, and then the child laughs, and you get a good picture! Thy will be done, Lord.

Tickled

Since we think of church as a serious place, if something funny happens, it seems doubly funny. I have been told that I have a high threshold of pain, but when it comes to getting tickled about something, I know my threshold is very low. Laughter is my safety valve. I'll explode if I hold it in. I'm a firm believer in the idea that suppressing laughter causes explosive reactions that can damage the organs. There have been times when I have done everything possible to try to keep from laughing. The more I tried, the more the pressure built up until I felt I would physically rupture. The worst of it is that sometimes it isn't all that funny.

Once we were in an afternoon meeting, and the speaker was droning on and on. Ahead of me sat a very, very large man in a white shirt. The sun was shining across some lady's face making a silhouette on his back as though it were a large screen. That wasn't so funny, but the lady would wrinkle up her nose, wipe it, scratch her head, and perform other such acts. My daughter and I soon lost control. I'm sure no one else would have had a clue as to what was funny. I would do my best to get control. As the man's back was in line with the speaker, I would look up only to see another act. I would talk harshly to myself and regain a measure of control, only to be unglued again by a snicker out of my daughter. We were no help to each other and were soon wiping away tears.

I don't believe men have the same mechanism. My husband never seems to have this problem. His nudging me to rebuke me only makes matters worse. One time, I was so out of control he was about to die of embarrassment. I got up and went downstairs to the bathroom, leaned over the sink, and laughed until I cried. By the time I returned, I had pretty well conquered my problem.

Once, this happened during Sunday school. The Sunday school book clearly had a misprint that anyone who had read the lesson ahead of time would have picked up on. It was a verse that is commonly known, and the mistake was glaring, so when the guy behind me read it as it was printed, I was surprised. By him reading it the way it was printed, it made no sense and was very funny. I wonder if he was thinking, *Should I read it the way it is, or read it the way I know it's supposed to be?* To my shame, it hit me as terribly funny. Out of respect, I tried to control myself, but I was tired and that makes my pressure valve really weak.

I put my head down and tried to think serious thoughts. But the pressure began to build and build! I held it in until I had to gasp for breath. A lady ahead of me was having the same problem. She told me later that she could make it until she heard me gasp for breath. I shook all over, wiped the tears away, and sometimes snorted. Again, my husband tried to control me. It just didn't work. The guy who had read it saw me laughing and thought it funny too, but that did not ease my feeling of guilt.

Feeling guilty only makes the problem worse. I hate when that happens, but Proverbs 15:13 says, "A merry heart maketh a cheerful countenance." I'm afraid I have a cheerful countenance way too many times, including at my own grandmother's funeral, when a bug made its painful way up the wall. No, it isn't that funny. I just can't help how I am wired. One cannot control when a laugh will come on. You don't look at your watch and say, "In five seconds, I am going to laugh." Luke 6:21 tells us about being blessed if you are weeping now, "for ye shall laugh." Laughter doesn't make you forget or dismiss your suffering, but it helps you survive it and get through it.

I find it interesting also the way people laugh. I tell my one friend I could be in downtown New York in a dark alley and hear him laugh, and I would know it was him. When one girl

I know laughs, it makes me think of a ping-pong ball bouncing on a table.

Once, my uncle was in a small church that was equipped with wooden chairs. The congregation got on their knees for prayer during the service. When they got up and my uncle sat on the chair, it collapsed. At first, everyone was sympathetic. Then he sat on the second chair, and it broke too. When he sat on the third chair and it broke also, they dismissed church. My uncle was not hurt, but the congregation couldn't get control of their laughter. I wasn't there, thank the Lord. Seeing it was in the Lord's house, you have to wonder, knowing God sees everything, why He allows some things to happen. Might He have a sense of humor that we have not accounted for?

Chapter Seven

Dogs Do Laugh!

Tip

I don't know how early in life one learns to love or, as in my case, be afraid of dogs. Our old farm dog was probably the most faithful animal that ever lived. My aunt always said that old Tip would have stood between my dad and a mountain lion. I grew up loving that dog, but he got old. My parents sold the farm in the middle of Kansas to move to the big city of Colorado Springs. Daddy told us children we would have to say good-bye to Tip. He felt it would be unkind to take our farm dog who was used to roaming everywhere, and tie him up on a city lot. It was a sad day when we gave him our last hugs and pulled away leaving Tip lying on the front porch. We children didn't know that Daddy had arranged for the neighbors to feed Tip until he had settled us into our new home and returned a week later for the farm auction. He would then take care of Tip in the most humane way he could think of.

When Daddy returned to the farm alone, who should come

out to meet him with such joy and love, expressed by his whole body and tail wiggling, but old Tip? Daddy told us later he could not have him put away, so he tucked Tip under a rocking chair in the back of his truck to make the eight-hundred-mile trip to Colorado. Daddy would stop periodically and check on Tip, but he made the trip like a trooper. I am not sure who was happier, the dog or the five of us children. Perhaps God felt we children had enough to adjust to going from farm life to city life and was using that old dog to ease our pain. That was the only dog in my life I ever really trusted.

Dog Chase!

Not all farm dogs are created equal. I had never been really friendly with our neighbors' old collie but was reasonably unafraid of him. It was when they got a new dog, and Pat, the neighbor girl, wanted me to see it, that I became fearful of dogs. Now what farm people would want with a puny, little, skinny white dog was more than I'll ever know. But on the other hand, why should I have been scared of that puny, little, skinny white dog either? I don't know how it happened, but somehow, a chase started. I was running for my life; the dog was in hot pursuit. I ran for the garage and so did the dog. I ran around the garage, and the dog did, too. I ran around the woodpile, and the dog did as well. Good thing it was a scrawny little dog! I was outrunning him! Pat was watching and began to laugh. Every time we made a round, I'd yell, "Pat! Get your dog!" And she would laugh harder.

I don't know how many rounds we'd made or how many times I'd yelled for her to get her dog, when Pat's mother heard the commotion and came out of the house. By that time, Pat had collapsed onto the woodpile holding her sides and was laughing so hard she couldn't talk. Around I went again with that stupid little animal's legs a white blur after me. I was a strong farm girl, raised on our own meat, eggs, milk, and garden, but my strength was waning. Pat's mother called the dog off and scolded Pat for letting it happen. I forever lost all respect for small, ratlike dogs and a good bit for Pat, also. Although I'm still not brave with dogs, I know now had I turned on him, the chase probably would have gone the other way.

Sometime after that, I was with another neighbor girl when she and I went to her uncle's farm. Why her mother would drive us there and not see to our safety, knowing they had a vicious dog—I just don't have an answer. But I do know my trust in dogs received another blow. Nancy wanted to show me something out behind the house. We started, but she said, "We need to be careful. Uncle Glen has a dog that will bite!"

Oh no! I thought. *What are we doing here?*

No sooner had she said it, than here he came, and he was bent on protecting all property involved. Nancy saw him coming and froze. The dog stopped and growled. I saw the hair on his back rise like the spiked hairdos of our modern days. With a scared, drawn-out voice, Nancy slowly said, "Oooooh, Smokey." She then made a dash, and jumped up on the hood of her mother's car. I didn't know what to do, but I had outrun Pat's dog; perhaps I could this one, also. I was a fast runner and could beat everyone in school except for one really fast boy named Keith, so I headed for home, which was three miles away.

I was making good progress, but this was no wimpy little

Chihuahua. It was a huge, no-breed mongrel. He was gaining on me, and I took the road, which made a right angle. His conscience didn't direct him to stay on the road, and he jumped the ditch, taking a shortcut. He almost had me when Nancy's uncle got the dog's attention by calling loudly and throwing his gloves ahead at the dog. Her uncle took my hand and led me back, while the dog strutted beside us, proud of his accomplishment. I vowed never to trust a dog again.

Yes, I know that was probably my own fault, but how does a child know that? I'm still scared even when the owner stands there and says, "She won't hurt you!"

Oh yeah? I have something written on my forehead that only dogs can read. It says, "Hey, doggie, want to have some fun? Watch this gal retreat! You'll never get done laughing. You'll have lots of stories to tell around doggie campfires!" They know! I *declare*, they just know! I am a grown woman and talk severely to myself, "Now they said it won't bite. Believe it." But it still comes through, and what really makes me mad is when they say, "Well, Fou-fou has never acted that way before." I declare when they weren't looking, I saw that dog snicker over my discomfort. It's bad enough to know that dogs have scared you and will be laughing about it and telling their offspring, but having your friends hysterically laugh too is just too much—especially when, as in Pat's case, they could have done something about it.

Once I was walking my friend to her house when we met a boy carrying three small dogs. All three dogs read my forehead, agreed to have some fun, and somehow jumped out of his arms. One came snapping at my heels, so I whirled and kicked at it. Wrong move! Another came from the other side. The faster I moved, the more the dogs became bent on biting me. The boy was distraught and tried to get ahold of them. He was grabbing and yelling and would get one, but while trying to hold it and gather up the others, it would escape again. It was a gravel street, and pebbles and dust were flying. Again, my friend deserted me, and from half a block away, I heard her gales of laughter. She said later she had never seen such fast tap dance moves, as I kept three (again small and white) mutts at bay. I still don't know how he got all three of those little ankle biters back into his arms. I was exhausted and saw those dogs grin as he gave me his sincere words of apology.

Don't Look up, Doggie!

When I had children of my own, I determined they would not fear dogs like I do, so I left all doggie introductions to my husband. I don't think he fears any dog. As our children were growing up, we had a home business of reupholstering. That meant that I often went to see a piece of furniture to give an estimate. When my daughter was two years old, I went to a place that I was sure must have a large dog. I could see nose prints on the storm door, and the altitude of those nose prints was uncomfortably high.

"Please, Lord, make it a little, scrawny—yeah, even white— varmint I can kick at." I gave my daughter a very reassuring speech about not acting like she even saw the dog. "Don't move fast. Don't scream. Don't be afraid!" Sure! Mommy's scared to death already. So holding her little hand in my already trembling one, I rang the doorbell. All my anticipated fears were fully grounded as a series of ferocious, deep barks erupted.

I held my foot against the storm door lest some unwitting person go ahead and let the dog out. With a pasted-on smile, I steadied my voice and very sweetly quipped, "I am here to look at your couch. She and I are uncomfortable with dogs." *More like absolutely paranoid!* I thought. "I just wondered if you could perhaps put the dog somewhere else."

What did I expect? Of course! "Oh, he won't bite a flea." Same old song—second verse! But I insisted, so they put the dog in the basement. Great help! That's where the couch was! I encouraged my little girl to stay right there and watch the blaring TV while I ran down to see the couch. At least it would only be my life and not both of ours. My nerves were stretched so tight they'd make strings on a violin look like jump ropes! I hated leaving my two-year-old with strangers, but when I looked down that flight of stairs and saw the glowing eyes of that dog, I was convinced I had chosen the lesser of two evils.

Never had I done a business deal so fast. I was hurrying to get out of there. As the lady was writing a check, her husband was determined to prove to me the sweetness of his dog. As he brought the dog back up, I gathered my trembling daughter in my own trembling arms. I started softly talking in her ear, "It's all right, honey. The doggie won't hurt you." *This is only a German shepherd that hit me at the waist, and your legs are hanging below that.* "Don't worry, Mommy's got you!" Great comfort! Mommy's about to faint!

The man said, "See, I'll put this rubber band over his muzzle. He can't bite." That only made the dog mad. "She can get down; he won't hurt her."

I wanted to scream, "Do you have a problem with leaving that dog in the basement until we leave? And how long does it take to write a check anyway?" But instead, I sweetly said, "Oh, she is still scared."

Then I know that dog thought, *I'll give her a memory!* And what a memory it has been! He put his head under the skirt of my dress, sniffing at my legs. The pervert! The man, trying to be funny, said, "Don't look up, doggie"! But look up he did! Actually, he stood up on his back legs with his paws on me, and his head still under my dress. I died two deaths right there! One of fear and the other of total embarrassment! That morning, I had put on a pair of dark pantyhose that had some runs in them. But those runs were above "see level" with my long skirt. No more! I was afraid to make a fast move to put my skirt down, and I wanted to scream. It seemed that moment froze into a half hour, though I know it was only seconds. Finally, we escaped, check in hand, and I backed my car out of the driveway. I drove a block away before I burst into tears. I vowed I'd never go back. We just didn't need the business so much that it would be worth that. But my husband talked me into going with him to pick up the couch. I got a babysitter for the children. And yes, my husband played with and petted the dog, which only made me feel more like a fool. Billy said he didn't see it, but I saw that dog look at me several times and grin. I hated him. Oh yes, too, my daughter just informed me that that is where she acquired her fear of dogs. Thanks to Mom!

Not so "Lucky"

Dogs do show expression. Just listen to this one. My sister had a dog named Lucky. No way did the name fit, except that he was just lucky to be called a dog and get his daily portion of food and love. He was a poor excuse for a dog. You couldn't keep him in a pen, and he barked at his own shadow. Not good characteristics for a city dog.

Well, one day, the UPS man arrived just as some of us were picking up a grill for a family picnic. The UPS man got out of his truck, and Lucky jumped out of his pen, barking loudly. The man quickly returned to his truck and called out, "You'll have to restrain that dog!"

My sister called back, "Don't worry. Lucky won't bite you for anything."

The UPS man called back, "That's what they all say, and I have been bitten by more dogs 'that wouldn't bite' than any other. Either he is gone or I can't deliver this package." I instantly felt a bond with that UPS man. I wasn't close enough to see if I could read the writing on his forehead, but I knew it was there!

Our visiting cousin who was around fourteen years old and very tall and obese decided to take after Lucky. Charlie's size alone would evoke fear, but when Lucky heard Charlie lumbering in close pursuit, you could see abject terror written on the dog's face. They made several laps around the yard. My sister started calling commands. She may as well have been speaking Greek to a two-year-old. That dog had a mind of his own. Finally, the dog decided that the porch would be a safe place. En route, however, he hopped onto the slanted metal cellar door located next to the porch. He was slipping and sliding, and the rapid churning of his legs got him nowhere, allowing his pursuer to gain ground. Just then, he gave a nervous glance over his shoulder and saw Charlie closing in. Abject terror registered on Lucky's face. With one last desperate lunge, his front paws caught the edge of the porch. With his back paws churning like fan blades to get traction, he jumped and finally landed on the porch. Again, you could see terror on his face as he turned and saw Charlie coming. His only hope was back in the pen. And back in the pen he went!

It only lasted a couple of minutes. Charlie collapsed on the porch panting for breath, the UPS man delivered the package, and eventually Lucky went to the happy hunting ground, but our laughter has lasted these many years, mainly because of that dog's obvious expressions. Truthfully, it is not my imagination, I have seen dog's faces show these emotions!

I take the scripture seriously in Philippians 3:2. "Beware of dogs," and a few other things. But "Beware of dogs" was first. I just have to stop there, and thank the Lord for the warning that seems necessary for me, if not for everyone else. I have often been told that all scripture doesn't apply to all, and I am convinced. But as for me, this is sufficient. I must take it seriously as it is a bit too late to teach this old dog, new tricks.

Chapter Eight

Why Am I at the Right Place at the Wrong Time?

Scared to Death

We use the expression so often, "I was scared to death!" I wonder how many people really have died just because they were scared. For instance, when an airplane is going down, I wonder how many died before it ever hit the ground. I'm sure I would. Or even in a road accident, say you see the truck coming, and you just die of fear. Who would ever know? Yeah, the body was mangled, but they died before the body ever felt a thing. I'm sure I could accomplish that. I just thank the Lord He has spared me from some situations, knowing how I am.

I say all that to say this—I came mighty near dying of fear once. I awakened from a nap and realized I needed to be at work soon. I got up, still groggy, and started down our driveway toward my car, which was parked on the street. I know I must've been still half asleep, when I raised my head to see a man on our porch. The daze I was in was gone instantly! This was not just any man, but a man who had murdered another just two days before. My only family member home was one of my sisters, and she was asleep. I was in an instant panic!

Although this guy and his brother rented one of my parents' apartments, we certainly didn't know them very well. And we surely didn't intend to get to know them better after reading last night's news. According to the newspaper, he had gotten into a drunken brawl down on a main street of town the night before and had killed a man.

My foggy little brain could only think that here is this man intent on murder, and I am next. Adding to my fear was the obvious huge fresh gash down across his forehead. He was sewed up like a baseball. He came down off the porch and straight for me. He smiled and held out a fist of money and said, "I have come to pay my rent."

Ever heard the expression, "her eyes were as big as saucers"? I could literally feel my eyes growing big in my sockets. I couldn't stop it! My skin was painfully stretching.

The expression, "my tongue turned to rubber," became a reality. I tried to say, "You'll have to talk to my mom and dad," but I blubbered so badly, he had to think I was severely handicapped. I blabbed like a drunk. "I … I … think m-m-my mom-mom-mom wants to-to-to … you … you need to-to c-come back wh-when my-my-my da-dad is here."

I wonder he didn't laugh. But he said, "Hey, I trust you; here's the rent. You can give it to your parents."

I blabbed some more and took note of another expression we

use: "My knees were knocking together." Mine were not just knocking; they were absolutely smiting one another, and I was helpless to stop it. Another expression, "white as a sheet"—well, I did that to. My sister said she suddenly had a feeling I was in trouble. She got up and pulled back the curtain to look out. She said there was positively no color at all in my face and my eyes were way too big.

I'm sure it only lasted a few minutes, but it seemed like forever. I blabbed enough to convince him to come back later. The truth is he was probably convinced that I was totally incapable of handling the money, much less getting in that car and driving to work. I can only be glad that he didn't make any quick moves or yell, "Boo!" I know I would not have lived to tell it. In extreme weakness, I made it back into the house.

When the guy arrived that evening, my dad answered the door and asked him about what we had seen in the paper. The guy explained that, although he was in on the fight, his brother was the one who had committed the murder. We didn't know the difference between the brothers.

I have been scared a lot of times since, but never to that extent. With age comes a bit of wisdom. But as a young girl, all I knew was this man had murdered someone, and I was the next one in line. I have also learned to trust Jesus, and that my times are in His hands. It is a comfort to know that He knows those dates on the tombstone which state the date of the birth of one and when the end will be. Yes, I was all of the expressions—white as a sheet, teeth chattering, knees knocking together, eyes big as saucers, scared to death ... well, make that almost to death.

The Restroom Gnome

I've just done it again! I believe I could safely declare that no one on earth has ever had so many unusual experiences doing a perfectly normal thing—using the restroom. I drove my husband to work and planned to spend the day in that area. I had not yet had my coffee or the small glass of milk with which I take my morning arthritis medicine. Yes, like a good little girl, I had gone to the bathroom before I left, but all of a sudden, I needed to use the bathroom. I have learned that when the warning lights come on, I'd better be finding a restroom.

My plans were to go through the drive-through at McDonald's and get my morning cup of coffee. I'm usually very stiff in the mornings, but with my medications and a little time, I limber up. I was hurting all over just thinking about dragging myself into McDonald's, clear to the back to the bathroom, and back out again. Then there came a wonderful thought! This dear little town has public restrooms in a convenient location. These were made to accommodate the Amish, who come to town in buggies. I could park in the alley right beside the building and only have to walk about nine feet with my crutch. My pain level was high, and I was happy to think of this and happier yet to find it warm and clean.

Just when I thought the emergency was over, I realized I could not get the door open to leave. I had noticed when I entered that it was heavy. I'd had to push with all my weight to get it open. Not only was it hard open, but it had a slick, perfectly round, stainless steel ball for a doorknob. I just didn't have the strength in my hands to turn the knob and pull at the same time. I struggled for at least fifteen minutes before I started yelling for help. Even with my strongest pull, I could only crack the door about a quarter of an inch—not enough to squeeze my crutch into. There was nothing to use to try to pry it open. I had left my cell phone in the car. So yell I must! I'm not able to stand very long, and the only place to sit down was the commode. So I yelled some more. It was seven in the morning, and I knew it might be hours before some Amish lady came to town in her buggy and needed to use a restroom. I kept calling for help for a half hour. At last, the door was timidly cracked open, and I could see a large man standing outside with another behind him. He said, "Were you calling for help?" By that time, I was so stressed yet relieved, I burst into tears and gushed all over them for rescuing me.

I felt God answered my prayers for rescue, but my daughter sure gave me a severe speech about always having my cell phone with me. "Someone could be in there waiting for you, and with your weak crippled condition—" Well, on and on she went!

I said, "Heather, for Pete's sake, this is Sugar Creek, not Cincinnati!"

"Yes," she said, "but had you had your cell, you could have called for help, and, you never know, sometimes people in little towns have said, 'Nothing like this has ever happened here'! It's all right to trust God—but just make it a little easier for Him. You're working your guardian angels overtime!"

Sometimes I have wondered what in the world Jesus ever wanted with me. And one time, I even asked Him, "What do You see in me that would make You want me for your child?"

He actually answered me quite audibly with some questions, "Who made you?"

I answered, "You, Lord!"

Again, He asked, "Do you not think that I made you and delight in you? Do you think I made a mistake?"

I was humbled as I muttered, "Sometimes, Lord, I have to wonder, but thank You for loving me anyway."

I have often said I think the Lord was laughing out loud when He made me. He has to have a sense of humor. Once I saw a *Far Side* cartoon of God making the world. It showed the earth and God's hand shaking a salt shaker onto it. The caption said, "Now, for just a few nerds." I don't really want to be a nerd, but I have to admit, sometimes, I seem just a bit different from my friends.

Another time the restroom gnome made its appearance was when our daughter brought her future husband home for the first time to meet us. Her cousin, in college also, brought her future husband as well, and we were all getting together for a lovely meal and a hay ride. Knowing I've embarrassed my daughter so many times, I vowed to watch my every move and make a good impression on this lovely young man. I did all right. All was going so well until I needed to use the restroom. I went to the one just off the sitting room where everyone was. There was a small child there, so I locked the door. I was having a lot of trouble with my hip at the time and didn't know that it needed to be replaced. The commode was not a handicap-accessible one, and when I got on, I could not get off. I quietly called Heather's name. She heard me and came to the door. I told her it was locked but to go to Aunt Sarah and see if she had some method of unlocking it. Well, they tried, but nothing seemed to work. One by one, the men got involved. Before all was said and done, they ended up taking the door apart. Everyone knew what was going on, and they were all having a good time laughing about it.

When I finally came out, I was so embarrassed. I was so disgusted with myself and said, "Honest to John!" I wasn't trying to be funny, but everybody collapsed. Nice try on making a good impression for Heather. The young man became my son-in-law and still laughs about his first impressions. Perhaps I had forgotten to pray about this meeting and was working so hard in my own strength.

I did pray about my daughter's wedding. I wasn't the one who did the bummer that time. It was *his* mother. When we were at the church for the rehearsal, it was she, not I, who backed into the emergency button on the elevator that called the local fire station. It gave me a bit of relief to know I was not the only one who seemed to be always bringing the house down. God was so kind in hearing my prayer and keeping His hand over my mouth and His arm around my shoulders, making it a lovely, unforgettable day.

The Seat

It seems I so often get into difficulties when I'm trying to help someone, but then again, I live in difficulty. I'd like to think that it's because I'm always helping someone, but I have friends who are known for their generosity and kindness, and they never seem to have the problems I do. I sometimes wonder if I have an angel who is supposed to be watching out for me, and she's taking time off, or maybe she is just plain worn out from watching me. I would love it if she could just ease some of the situations a bit.

If you have a pickup truck, you can rest assured when someone needs to move, your number will be dialed. Such was the case with a dear older lady of our church. Lots of us really pitched in and saw to it that she was relocated in another part of town. We did something then that we would never do now: we loaded the truck to the limit and then rode on the tailgate as we made the trip between houses. Amazing how time changes things. Young people today have no idea the fun they have missed, or rather the embarrassment.

With one of the loads, my friend and I were perched on the tailgate, as my husband headed up through town. Because of the big load, he could not possibly see us. All was going well until the lid off a portable commode slid off and hit the pavement. The people in a car behind us saw it and wanted to help. They stopped, picked it up, and rushed to try to catch up with us. They tried to wave us down, but my husband could not see them and went on speeding through town. We just made it through a stoplight, and they had to stop. I was glad; perhaps we could shake them and forget about the whole thing. The last thing I wanted to be concerned about was the ring of a pot lid. But the people did not give up. We were detained at a stoplight, and here they came rushing up behind us. The lady jumped out waving the lid as she hurried to get it to us before my husband took off again. She didn't make it, jumped back in the car, and raced after us again.

At last, we both got stopped at the same light. I have often wondered what the people around thought. I hoped they thought it was a picture frame. I thought about holding it up to my face like one to make them believe it. My husband took off again, so I looped the thing over my arm and hung on, waving thanks to them. When we got to our destination, we told my husband about the circus he had missed. He hadn't seen a thing. The angel who was supposed to be watching me was probably so busy making sure I didn't fall off the tailgate that she never thought I might be embarrassed over a commode lid. I'm thankful it was the lid that fell and not me. Still, I don't see why it couldn't have been a picture frame!

My Attempt at Being Cool

One of our daughter's college friends from out of state came to see her. They hadn't seen each other since college days and decided to take in some of the beautiful scenery around us and then eat at a special restaurant. They so sweetly invited me to go along. I knew I would really enjoy the outing but did not want to be viewed as an intruder, so I crawled in the backseat and kept a low profile. I only spoke when I saw something I felt they might miss or would lend interest to the trip.

After the noon meal, the day wore on, and they got to talking less and fell into a mindless chewing and cracking of gum. Now when I was a child, a stick of gum was a rare treat, usually received as a highly treasured prize for some notable accomplishment. Also, we were taught the catechisms of chewing gum—mouth closed, not in public, never when speaking, and never, never, on the pain of death, in church! As for making a crack, that was unheard of in decent places! That was strictly reserved for that big pink bubble gum given at birthday parties. Those were the laws of gum.

So, as I sat watching these two loudly chewing and popping the gum, I was glad that at least we were in the car by ourselves. Where had I gone wrong, not to have trained my daughter better? But the more I observed, I saw how free and relaxed they were. Perhaps I had been misled as a child. How curbed, deprived, perhaps even abused I was not to have been able to use the gum for what it may have been invented for—a carefree time! Along with the cracks, they were blowing huge balloons and taking them effortlessly back into their mouths. Boy, what fun! I remember trying that once as a child and getting it stuck in my long hair. Mother had to give me a short crop to right the situation. I'm older now, and know what I'm doing. How accomplished I might feel if I were to blow a big bubble and successfully retrieve it. Long overdue! So without a word to them, I tried. I say, I *tried*! It ended up as a sort of explosion, and the whole wad blew far from my mouth and stuck to the side of the driver's window, narrowly missing his ear. First, I got a shocked look and then convulsions of laughter.

"Hey, that was cool."

Cool? In my day, that meant you were chilly. I was anything but chilly. I had plenty of heat in my face. I feared for my life as the car careened about as he tried to control himself. I reached up, retrieved my gum, replaced it in its original wrapper, and then slunk back into my seat. All the rest of the day, they would bring up the act and laugh all over again. So much for my being "cool." Lord, deliver me from being cool. I was just trying to have fun.

Chapter Nine

Having Kids Doubles Your Joys and Your Gray Hairs!

Be careful little mouth what you say

We have two awesome children, but my husband has often said, "Perhaps we should have stayed with raising radishes." Somehow, the books on parenting just don't cover all the things that could happen with the raising of children. I'm sure I was a terror to my parents and fully understand now why we celebrate Mother's and Father's Days. It has been said that having children starts with labor and never quits. Once a mother, always a mother. I'm sure I could be in my coffin and someone nearby could call, "Mom!" and I would sit up. They can bring you so much joy and also so much embarrassment.

When our oldest was a mere lad, he would say our pastor's wife's name so cutely. One time, when the pastor and his wife were here, I did my best to get Alan to say, "Mrs. McKay."

Try as I would, I could not get him to say it. Finally, he

looked up and very loudly said, "Outhouse!" Where that came from, I have no idea. I don't think he even had the concept of what an outhouse was. But then I suppose I didn't do much better, when around the same time, we went out to eat and I mortified myself. I had been reading way too many Dr. Seuss books—at least that is my excuse. When the waitress asked me what I wanted, I answered, "Roast beast." My husband gave me a startled, wicked grin. He can just be glad that I had not added, "Who hash." Remember Dr. Seuss's roast beast and who hash?

"...hands what you do..."

Our son grew up to become a jack-of-all-trades. He was about sixteen years old when he was helping the carpenter who was building an addition to our home and had a serious accident. At the time, I was uptown taking care of an elderly lady. The phone rang with someone from the local hospital telling me I needed to get to the hospital soon to sign some papers, as my son had been involved in an accident and they needed my signature. They sounded so calm, I didn't think it could be too bad. After I had taken the elderly lady to the bathroom, I suddenly remembered that the guy Alan was working with was not one to hurry off to a doctor. If he had indeed taken Alan to the hospital, this could be serious.

I rushed over to the hospital and found Alan lying in the emergency room white as a sheet. His hand was lying on his chest, with part of one finger missing. On a tray beside him lay the rest of his finger. The nurses were watching me closely in fear that I would faint. I didn't faint, but I started crying and couldn't seem to stop. Alan reached out with his good hand, patted me, and said, "Mama, don't worry; I am in God's hands." What more could a mother want?

I implored the doctor to try to put the rest of his finger back on. The doctor, however, felt it was not wise, as it would always be dead. I pleaded that he was a piano player. The doctor asked if he did that for a living. No, it wasn't that. My mind just couldn't wrap around the fact that one finger would be missing so much. Two of his other fingers had a good bit of damage but would be okay.

As it was, after a time, he was still able to play the piano. I still have a hard time looking at that finger. He, however, has had fun with it. In college, he would hollow out the end of a wiener, fill it with ketchup, and place it over his shortened finger. He would wait until the girls at his table were ready to eat their dessert and then act like he had bitten off his finger and the blood was running. They would leave the table very quickly, leaving him their desserts. I still cannot see the humor in that. But maybe this was one way of making the best of the situation.

"...eyes what you see..."

Our daughter loved her doll. It was a gift given to her for her first birthday by my parents. It was the size of a small baby and looked very realistic. From that time on, that doll went with her everywhere she went. She even named it Precious Cute. Sometimes, I would get disgusted having to wait while she saw that Precious Cute had on the proper clothing, complete with a coat and hat. Every week, when we went shopping for groceries, the doll had to go along. People would look at me like, "Why would that woman let that small child carry the baby?" The doll's head had little support of its own, like a real baby's, making the situation look realistic. I finally got used to people looking and then eventually getting the idea that it was a doll and not a real baby. Even as she got older, that doll could *not* be left at home alone. What was really embarrassing though was when she wanted to go to the restroom and laid the doll on top of the groceries I already had in the cart and left. Here comes this thirty-year-old woman pushing a cart with her baby lying on the groceries. Again, I got lots of looks, until I explained it was my daughter's doll. A couple times of that, and I put an end to the restroom trips.

The compassion she had for her doll has carried through into her life on every level. From her early childhood, other little people have been drawn to her. I don't know if it is the look in her eyes or what, but children have always been and are still drawn to Heather. She has something that I do not have. She is so gifted in children's ministry and teaching school.

One day, as we were driving down the street, I saw two little boys and was about to say, "Look at those little urchins!"

I was glad I kept my mouth shut for at least the count of five, because just that quickly, she said, "Mama, aren't they precious?"

I'll have to admit I did not see what she saw but quickly changed my attitude. Doesn't the Bible say something about a child shall lead them? My children have taught me many things.

The Lake

I hate my short memory, but there is a scene that I would like to forget but can't. Heather had come home from college one Friday afternoon in early May. Every year, we plan a little outing where we go about fifteen miles away to a privately owned little cabin that sits upon the bank overlooking a small, beautiful lake. Although we usually do it in the summertime, the weather was beautiful, and we decided to go out that evening and stay overnight. It was a bit cool, so we built a fire in the woodstove in the cabin, and a fire outside to cook over. Just before dusk, Heather said, "Daddy, let's go take a boat ride."

He said, "Good idea. I'll take my pole and see if I can catch a fish or two before dark."

I sat by the fire with my feet propped up and watched them cross the lake. Although this place is not far off the beaten track, it is back in far enough that you hear very little of the outside world. It was one of those evenings that was probably as close to heaven as one could get on earth. But that suddenly changed when they started back and were almost to the shore. Heather had taken in the whole ride facing her father who was fishing off the back of the boat. The people who own this tiny resort always keep the boat docked on the earth dam, which is also the deepest part of the lake. Heather suddenly decided to turn around and watch where they were going to dock. It was just a little rowboat, and somehow, when she turned around, it unbalanced everything. Quicker than it takes to tell it, that boat flipped upside down.

I knew Heather could not swim, and although my arthritis had me pretty well handicapped, I jumped up and ran down to the lake as fast as I could go. I screamed and screamed, hoping to attract the attention of someone who could come to help us. There was little hope of anyone hearing me, but I was doing my best with everything I could think of. En route, I saw a life preserver hanging on the side of the toolshed. It had a rope on it, and I grabbed it and rushed to the edge of the water. There, I saw Heather clinging to the side of the upside-down boat. My husband is a good swimmer but was out of sight. Later, I found out that as the boat turned over, it hit him on the head, knocking his glasses off, and when he came up, he was underneath the boat. He too was extremely concerned about Heather. He said he was so shocked when he came up and saw her still above water. The water was extremely cold, and Heather kept calling out, "Mama, I can't hold on! I can't hold on!"

I kept trying to throw that life ring as far as I could to reach them. All the time, I was calling to Heather to keep holding on. Sending up desperate prayers, I was finally able to throw the thing far enough my husband could reach out and get ahold of it. I pulled desperately and got them to shore. We hurried up to the cabin where they stripped out of their wet clothing by the woodstove. They were well-nigh frozen, and my husband couldn't talk. I took control, threw everything into the van, and started for home. I had the heater going as high as I could, until I could hardly breathe. Since we were just staying overnight, we had not taken a lot of extra clothes. My husband did not have what he needed, so I had made him put on one of my winter nightgowns. It wasn't until we were almost home that my husband came out of shock and said, "Please don't wreck this thing. I don't want to go to the hospital in this garb."

That Sunday was Mother's Day. In church, my daughter got up to sing, and I dissolved into tears. All I could think about was how close I had come to not ever hearing that beautiful voice again.

Just this week, in one of my art classes, a dear lady told us about having lost her son when he was twenty years old. Of course we asked for details, and she told us that he had gone into the woods to walk the dog, had fallen into a pond, and had not been found for two weeks. We ladies, of course, were all sympathetic, but I couldn't keep back the tears, as I related to her story. I would never want to go through something like that again, but perhaps it has made me more sensitive to others. I could feel her pain, at least to some extent. I hope I was able to reach out to her. I hope I put a drop of oil on her pain.

Oh, the things children say!

Whole books have been written on the cute things children say. Our children, of course, had their share. When Heather was little, she often got carsick. One day, as I was sitting at my sewing machine, she came to me and said, "Mama, I am homesick."

I could not figure that one out. I said, "What do you mean?"

She answered, "I feel like I do when I get sick in the car, but I am home." Pretty good reasoning really.

Our children were seven and eleven years old when we made a trip to Yellowstone National Park. Somewhere out West, we went into a convenience store and I saw some dishes there that were made to look like buffalo chips. I was expostulating about it: "Gross! Who would want dishes that look like buffalo chips?"

I was surprised to learn that our children didn't know what I was referring to. I gave a very detailed history lesson about the pioneers going West and how that they had used buffalo droppings, called chips, to make their campfires.

Later, as we were touring the park, we could see a lone buffalo quite some distance away. My husband was concentrating on driving and asked, "What is he doing?"

Without a second thought, our son innocently answered, "Daddy, I think he's chipping." He was not even remotely intending to be funny, but my husband and I certainly got laughter out of that one.

Children can be a trial at times, but they can also be a bright spot. The Bible holds great respect for children. One verse speaks of them being as arrows in a quiver; it says that the one who has a quiver full of them is blessed. I somehow feel our quiver was only big enough to hold two, and we are happy with our blessings. God always knows best and never makes a mistake.

Get to Bed!

It was one o'clock in the morning when my motherly instincts fairly threw me out of bed. I heard lots of giggling and laughter. At that time of the night, most mothers see very little as being funny. That was me. A friend of our son's had come to visit, and he, with our children, had gone out to visit with the children of a family in our church. My husband and I had gone to sleep knowing our children were with other church young people having a good time, playing their guitars and singing. They had returned, and it was now very late. It was high time for them to be in bed. I could not imagine what could be so funny, so I put on my robe and marched to the family room. When I arrived, no one said a thing. Our son, who was anything but small, tried to hide behind insufficient drapes. Just his feet were sticking out. Alan's friend, though his last name was Bigger, was anything but big. He stuffed his short, small frame under a Queen Anne chair. When I walked on into the room, he stuck his curly blond head out from under the chair, with purposely enlarged, frightened eyes. Acting like a scared puppy, who was about to get swatted with a newspaper, he rolled pleading eyes up at me, looking over the top of his dislodged glasses.

Neither boy said a word, but as though they had rehearsed the whole act, they seemed to know each move the other would make. They acted like frightened rabbits determined to escape me—mean old Mr. McGregor.

Our daughter was collapsed on the couch in gales of laughter, which only fueled their fire. All my resolve to straighten these kids out and send them to bed was gone. It was beyond description. They made humor movies look dull.

I too was in gales of laughter. There's something about the mix of being a mother, having had children, the early morning hours, and being tickled, that just doesn't go together well. I thought I would rupture and made a fast exit to the bathroom. Once there, I could imagine their antics had I not made it in time. They would have been crawling up on the furniture and acting as though they were escaping a flood. I finally returned to the silent movie and joined my daughter in her mirth, until finally exhausted, I ordered everyone to bed. Oh, the joys of children!

Christmas Caroling

I think there are some things that just come in the package of becoming a mother. Maybe not all mothers are alike, but so many times I have heard a mother say things like, "When I was a kid, I had to do without such and such, and my children aren't going to have to do that." Or I have heard declarations of, "My children aren't going to be like I was or like Aunt So-and-So, or have to do this or that." I'll have to admit I joined the club. "My children are going to grow up proper!" It wasn't that I didn't have a wonderful home; it just seemed like I was always bumbling things up. I hoped to spare my children some of my embarrassments. I soon learned there are some things you just can't control when you have children.

In our circle, we liked to do surprise Christmas caroling. Our children had taken voice lessons from a very special teacher for several years, and I thought it would be nice for our group to surprise the teacher one night before Christmas with a couple of songs. I could picture his delight in hearing good voices lifting the carols on the night air. I could see his face when he would flip on the porch light to discover some of his students there singing to him, using the talents he had helped develop.

We pulled up quietly with the headlights off, slipped out of the cars without slamming the doors, and headed for the porch. As we tramped through the snow, I encouraged our son and daughter to be at the head of the pack so when he looked out, he would recognize some familiar faces.

All was going well, until our son's snow-caked boots came in contact with a slick, painted wooden porch floor. Not only was there the thud from his falling, but his speed fetched him across the porch until his boots slammed against the screen door. The teacher was surprised all right—more like downright scared. He was just inside the window, and I can still see his eyes wide with concern as he headed for the door to turn on the porch light. By that time, the group had started to sing. Our son had righted himself, but many were laughing too hard to sing much. It took a while for the teacher to assimilate what was going on and enjoy the singing. I'm sure he was wondering why we had to announce our arrival with the blast of a shotgun.

Another time, we went to an elderly lady's home and slipped around to the back of the house. Right where we gathered to sing sat a commode that the lady would use in the summer as a flowerpot. Out of my control, this time, was my husband. He had a deer call for hunting in his pocket. He pulled it out, sat down on the commode, and blew. I was furious. Here I was trying to keep the children behaving properly, and my husband was the one upsetting the apple cart! Needless to say, the children were in stitches of laughter. They sang all right but with much mirth. I gave my husband a strong speech about making the children laugh when they should be taking their responsibilities seriously. I, however, was the one to eat humble pie later, when the lady sent a thank-you note to the church for our singing. In the note, she wrote how she had never seen such a happy group. I guess sometimes God has to bypass my wonderful ideas of how things should be to accomplish His will. That lady was blessed by such a happy group of singers. In spite of my properness, God used the circumstances at hand to lift the lady's spirit.

A Mother Forever

There are some things in life that once you start, you will never get done doing. One of my friends just told me, "Motherhood is terminal. Once you are one, you never get over it." Once a mother, always a mother! Even after the children have left home and are making a trip, she just wants to know when they have reached their destination. I still find myself telling the children things that they, being adults, already know or are planning on doing. My mother is not exempt. Sometime back, my sister with her husband and I with mine decided to take a one-day trip into the mountains to see a castle that was being built. We got into the car and were ready to leave, when Mother stepped out onto the back porch and called out, "You will want to use the restrooms as soon as you get there. They are on your right as you enter the parking lot."

I did not think anything about it until we started away and my brother-in-law said, "There isn't a one of us in this car under the age of fifty, and here she is telling us when and where to go to the bathroom!" We had a high time laughing about it and chalked it up to motherhood.

My mother was a seamstress and took pride in dressing us four girls in cute dresses, often alike. I was far more of a tomboy than my sisters and had to have been "a mother's nightmare."

I remember one Sunday when we all had new dresses and marched into church. Of course, the only dress that Mother had basted the sleeves into and forgotten to machine sew later would be mine. Wiggle worm that I was, I soon had the caps of the sleeves detached, leaving them only attached at the pits. I could look across my shoulders and see the tops of my sleeves standing out from my dress. I always had an overactive imagination, and I immediately believed I had angel wings. Angel wings were not made to remain in a folded position, so there I sat in church, out of Mother's reach, "flapping my wings."

Another time, she put the cutest little straw hats with long ribbons down the back on us girls. Somehow, my sisters were able to sit like little princesses. I could never get that title. I managed to press my back against the bench, pinching the ribbons, only to bow my head, and pop the hat off. The hat would fall behind the bench. I couldn't see that as a problem, so I would bail off the bench, reach under to retrieve the hat, and sit until the next unavoidable incident. I am well aware of why we celebrate Mother's Day. Some mothers definitely deserve more celebration than others. My mother would come in that class.

I wasn't all pain to my mother, however. Almost every summer, I would spend at least a week with my grandmother who lived in town. Once while I was there, one of her rich relatives from California came all the way to Kansas to see her. I felt pretty lucky to be there as he thought I was pretty special. When he went to leave, he gave me a great big fifty-cent piece. Back in those days, that was a lot of money. I asked Grandma if I could go to the dime store. It was only three blocks away, and she said yes. I skipped all the way to the store, planning what I would do with my money. I walked in and saw the candy counter. Right there in front were coconut bonbons, my mother's favorite candy. Mother would be happy with my buying candy for her. I had no concept of money, so told the girl I wanted some of those coconut bonbons. She asked how much I wanted. I had no idea, so I held out my money and said, "I want this much."

She gave me my candy and gave me some change. Boy!, was I happy. I had the candy and my money too. I skipped all the way back to the garden gate. When I got to the garden gate, I thought, *Oh, I could use all the rest of this money for candy and have some for myself.* So, without a word to Grandma, I turned around and skipped back to the store. When I got there, I held out my hand full of money and asked the girl to give me the rest of that in candy. She looked so surprised but accommodated me. Again, I skipped back to Grandma's. When I showed her what I had done, she put somewhat of a damp blanket on my enthusiasm. "You mean you spent all that money on candy?" Yes, I had, but I was happy because I had a gift for Mother. Coconut bonbons have always been special to me because of my gift to Mother, and I realized at a very young age the joys of giving. In Acts 20:35, Jesus' own words tell how blessed one will feel when giving. I can still remember the swelling of my little heart as I anticipated the moment I would give my gift to my mother. It meant even more to my mother coming from her daughter who was always a little more on the wild side.

Chapter Ten

Things Are Not Always as They Seem!

Is the Wash on the Line?

We live near an Amish community, and I have often been asked to drive them to various places. One family has a baby with special needs—really special needs. The dear little lamb has spent more of his days in the hospital than at home. They called me to take this tiny little boy back to the hospital for yet another procedure. It was a winter day, and they brought him out in his carrier, all covered with blankets, and placed him in the seat behind me. There is so much stuff to take when you go anywhere with a baby, but nothing compared to what they needed for this special little boy. Some of his many problems were that he could not eat, swallow, or even cry. A special machine had to be hauled wherever he went, to be used any moment he started struggling for breath. The trip was only an hour long, but in that hour, his mother turned on the machine and saved his life nine more times. At the hospital, they whisked him away, again covered with blankets, and told me to park the car and meet them at the cafeteria at noon.

At noon, I went through the line and took my tray to their table. There, they had the baby carrier set on the bench, and I got my first look at the baby. I sent up a desperate prayer, and the Lord graciously helped me to take control of my emotions.

On the way home that evening, the weary mother laid her head back against the headrest, only to be alerted again and again to use the machine for the baby. I asked her how often she had to do that, and she said at least every fifteen minutes through the night and all day long. I observed the father of the child reach around at times when the struggling was going on and take the baby's foot in his hand, reassuring the child that he was there.

I believe from the bottom of my heart that if a wee one like this child died, he would be carried through the pearly gates by a host of angels. No, probably, he would be skipping on his stubby little legs. So as we journeyed home, I began to pray.

"Lord, just take this little guy on to heaven. He will never have a life here. He has to be fed through a tube; he will probably never talk; he can't even cry. Lord, just take him out of this misery. The mother would only have to sleep through one time of him struggling, and he would be in glory. Lord, just take him."

I know I'm a bit impulsive and began to think that perhaps the Lord would quickly answer my prayer. After all, sometimes the Lord answers instantly. Then I began to pray, "Lord, please don't let me have an accident to accomplish Your will."

When we got back to their house, I realized I was the only one thinking like I was. The wash line was loaded with drying clothes flapping in the wind, and the dinner was prepared and on the table; all of this was accomplished by the older children left at home. When they saw us pull up, they came running outside, jostling one another to be the first to get the baby, shower him with kisses, and take him into the house.

When I drove away, I could not help but think of the love that was shown for that helpless little piece of humanity—the devotion of a mother to sacrifice not having even one good hour of sleep to see that he stayed alive, the father's loving touch when the child struggled for breath, the brothers and sisters doing extra chores so that their helpless little brother might live.

In my stunned silence, the Lord began gently talking to me. "Girl, I have some children too that make others uncomfortable. Some are far from perfect. Some are not very pretty, at times, disgusting. But, like that family, I love them. Yes, I work with them constantly, trying to get them to live a 'normal' Christian life. Yes, sometimes it is every fifteen minutes. (I was hoping He didn't mean me!) I don't give up on them or throw them out. I am love."

Then I begin to do some soul-searching. "Am I making someone sick? Am I self-centered, dogmatic, unloving, uncharitable, or anything that would be displeasing to you, Lord? Please keep sucking out that which would choke me and make me of no use. Please help me so that I am not always being that helpless baby, who can do little to help another. Let me be one of your children who will have the wash on the line and the dinner on the table. And, Lord, help me to be like the brothers and sisters (all a part of your family) blessed with unconditional love for one another."

The Wedding Dress

I am a seamstress and have made many wedding dresses for my customers. I am not keen on making a wedding dress a year before a wedding. Anything can happen: a death, a breakup, weight gain, who knows? One of my customers was a very organized girl, who wanted her dress made a whole year ahead of the date. The unthinkable happened—she gained weight. Who among us hasn't? The other day, she arrived at my door with that beautiful dress all in pieces—and I mean literally, pieces. She had thought she'd alter it, and no one would have to know she was a bit bigger than when I had made the dress. She had ripped—yes, *ripped*—the seams apart. I am really fussy about opening seams. It takes almost as good a seamstress to take something apart as to put it together. There's something dangerous about the word *rip*. In some places, she had cut the fabric. In one place, she had used too hot of an iron and scorched it. She knew a little about sewing, how to go forward and backward, but by the loopies beneath some of the seams, I realized the only thing she knew about tension was the tension she had gotten herself into.

In tears, she handed me the mess, and you never saw a more repentant, humble girl as she detailed her dilemma. Now, with the wedding only a month away, she was back to square one, with no wedding dress. I took the folded pieces that had very little resemblance to the original and put my arm around her. "Don't worry," I reassured her. "After all, I created it in the first place, so I can fix it." I took those pieces and reconstructed them. A little less seam here, an extra piece there, and a motif to cover the scorch, I worked at restoring the dress. It was perhaps a bit unorthodox (patterns just don't come with those extra pieces under the arms and so forth), but I soon had the dress fixed so only the most observant seamstress at the wedding would ever have guessed anything was unusual.

During those hours of working on the dress, I thought of my first words to her, "Don't worry, I created it in the first place." God, our Creator, sure gets some messes on His hands sometimes. Who has not thought, *"I can fix this!,"* when what we really need to do is take the whole mess to Jesus and drop it in His hands. I have seen people struggle for a lifetime with traits of self, always trying to do better and handle it, when they really need to haul the whole thing to Christ and let Him set the whole system right. The longer one tries to "fix" it without the Creator's help, the more messed up it becomes. Sin leaves scars. Many have let it go so long, that although God reconstructs their life, there are damages done that may be visible. God has to work at the job to heal those lifetime habits and broken families. Let's just turn the whole fabric of our lives over to Him early and leave it there. He alone can adjust us as we go through growing pains. He will always allow just enough ease and tightening to keep us looking like the image He wants us to have—a reflection of Himself. And, in the end, we will be fitted with the perfect wedding garment ready for that great wedding day.

Chapter Eleven

Food for Thought

Food

Without fail, we pretty much find ourselves at the table three times a day. I have often said if it weren't for eating, we would be rich. But don't a lot of pleasant memories gather around food? I am probably old enough to remember when chocolate drops first came out—those little tepee-shaped candies covered with chocolate. And ribbon candy? When we lived on a farm in Kansas, all the neighbors from miles around would gather at the old stone country church for a Christmas program. Any child who could talk would have a part. Even the most timid would brave it for that brown paper bag of candy that was waiting for them under the huge Christmas tree in the corner. Every piece was a treasure, and a lifetime has not erased the warm memories that are triggered when I see candies like those that were in that plain old brown paper bag.

It all brings up pleasant memories, family traditions, and even sometimes disasters. I never see a squashed loaf of bread but what I don't think of one of my mess-ups. Because my arthritis was paining me one day when I went shopping, I took the battery-operated shopping cart. I had picked up some bread, when I found a good bargain on meat. I stood up to get the meat but realized I did not want to squash the bread in the cart, so I took the bread out and laid it on the seat. I got so carried away with the bargains, I forgot the bread. Without thinking, I sat down and immediately thought, *What a nice, soft seat!* My brain kicked in, and I leaped back out of the seat. Need I say the bread looked like I might have baked it? When I bake, I can't seem to get anything to rise. The bread still tastes like bread; it just doesn't have the look it should. One of my sisters has always taken her bread, squashed it into a ball, and enjoyed it that way. Squashed bread doesn't make very good sandwiches, but it tastes all right dipped in jelly.

Shortly after we were married, I attempted making doughnuts. I got my Dutch mother-in-law's recipe, put all the things together, and worked all day trying to produce a masterpiece like hers. My husband called me at noon and asked what I was doing. I was so proud to let him know that I was being like his mother, making doughnuts. He said his mouth watered the rest of the day in anticipation of the doughnuts. When he came home, I told him, "Billy, look at the ceiling, think doughnut, and eat. They taste like doughnuts, smell like doughnuts, but look like onion rings." It's amazing how much we get hung up on the texture of things. They really did taste like doughnuts, and I'm sure they had as many calories, but for some strange reason, he was very disappointed.

I am sure our children's teacher will never forget an occasion with us when we took her out to eat. It was a buffet, and we had eaten our share when I decided to have a very small bowl of ice cream. I took the tiny bowl to the ice cream fountain and pulled down on the lever. For some reason, the thing got stuck and would not shut off. It kept spitting out ice cream, and I kept turning the bowl around and around to keep it from falling to the floor. I lifted on the handle, kicked the machine, and literally did everything I could to get it to shut off. Finally, someone came to my rescue and shut it off, but by that time, the ice cream was all of nine inches deep and hanging out all sides. I had already made a scene and was so embarrassed to carry that deep dish of ice cream back through the crowded dining room. The children's teacher was facing that direction and had seen the whole thing. She laughed until she cried. A waitress came along, not knowing what had happened, and gave me a disgusted look. Why me? Why do these things happen to me? Obviously, I do not plan them!

Once we were on a picnic with my husband's family, when they decided to roast marshmallows. I had one on the stick when it caught fire. I thought I could just give it a quick swish through the air to put out the fire. It put out the fire all right, but the marshmallow came off the stick and came down right on the end of my nose. I really thought we might have to take my father-in-law to the hospital for a laugh-induced heart attack. He well-nigh never recovered. He never forgot it either.

I love fruitcake now, but I didn't when I was a kid. After we moved to Colorado, a very dear elderly lady of the church sort of adopted us children as grandchildren. One day, as we were on our way home from school, she asked us in for a piece of fruitcake. I had never had it before, and somehow, it hit me wrong. We loved her dearly, and I didn't want to hurt her feelings, so I gradually slipped pieces of the cake down into my boot. I may have done it a little too fast, because she wanted to give me seconds. It was so sweet of her, but I just could not appreciate the taste. After we left and had walked several blocks, we stopped and I emptied my boots. I'm sure some birds had their own Christmas feast.

I don't profess to be a good cook. My husband's mother, in contrast, would be marked as one of the best cooks in the nation. That could make it a bit difficult for me, but my husband has only once said anything about the dishes I have prepared. That time was when I did something that was clearly out of my league. My friend had talked me into making a cheese soufflé. It came out just like it was supposed to. It was nice and fluffy, straight up out of the dish, and just like the picture showed. I, myself, had never had a cheese soufflé, so I did not know quite what to expect. We both ate some before he looked up and said, "Honey, could we just stay with things we can spell?" I was not impressed either. I called my friend, and she came over and ate the whole thing. It has been a joke in our family ever since about me only making things that we can spell.

My husband loves shrimp, but I can hardly take the smell of it. Once, we went to a restaurant, and he ordered shrimp. They brought much more than he could eat. One thing was for sure, I was not going to help him. Knowing how much he liked it though, I thought it would be a shame to throw it away. I wrapped it up in a napkin and put it in my purse. On the way home, I suddenly remembered that a men's store in town was having a special for Christmas. I wanted to get him a sweater and asked him to stop at the store and remain in the car. I found what I wanted and was so happy—that is until I went to pay for it. I had forgotten about the shrimp and had to paw past it to get to my money. The strong smell of fish wafted all through the air. Again, I was so embarrassed. I know that cashier has probably been telling for years about the woman who came in at Christmastime. There was something really fishy about her!

Chocolate-covered!

I love chocolate! What a weak way of saying that. Doesn't everyone like chocolate? One would have to have a severe problem not to, wouldn't one? Well, perhaps there are a few of us who have a severe problem the other way. We just love chocolate too much. At any rate, this is probably the one area where I struggle the most for self-control. When my family gives me a box of chocolates, they always say, "Just two a day. You are not allowed to eat the whole thing in one sitting!" How dumb! What would ever make them think of that?

Some years ago, our daughter went to a wedding that had a chocolate fountain at the reception. As she was taking the toothpick and carefully putting a strawberry under the chocolate, she said to my brother standing nearby, "I could never have one of these at my wedding." Of course, he wanted to know why. She said, "Because my mother would overdose and disgrace the whole family! No, she would probably be here with both hands cupped, burying her face in it. Forget about greeting the guests … Mom … Well, she is over there glued to the chocolate fountain."

But one needs to understand, everything would taste better with chocolate on it. My children declare that I would eat a worm, if it were covered with chocolate. Fortunately, they have not tried that one on me. They're good kids. They might try a gummy worm, however. Just days ago, my husband read in the newspaper where one can go and get a bath in chocolate. He said, "Hey, honey, here's something that might interest you!" Of course, he was joking. Why would anyone want to have a bath in something so wonderful? I am *not* into drinking bathwater!

I suppose I would be the only one to think of it, but isn't that kind of like God's presence? He pours His grace, love, and power over the circumstances of our lives, covering us with a sweetness that far exceeds chocolate. Even a turnip might taste good covered with chocolate. Thus, even the not-so-nice things in our lives, when covered with the Holy Spirit, are so much more tolerable, maybe even almost delicious.

We will have sorrows and pain in our lives, but if we are covered with God's warm presence, we can endure and perhaps even relish those times of sweet communion with Him.

I especially refer to when my father died. He was the hub of the family and the glue that drew extended family members together. I knew the time was coming when he would be leaving us and was sure I would be a basket case. God enveloped me in His warm presence to a point I never dreamed one could feel. Chocolate covered? There is no comparison. The good things, and the bad things, when dipped fully in God, make life richer than any of the richest chocolate. I feel the warm flow, just talking about it!

Chapter Twelve

Just Slipping In

The Rabbit

There is one thing that I have learned through experience, and that is that I should never plan on "just slipping in" anywhere—you know, those times when you need to be present but just want to play low key and slip in and back out without much ado?

One such time was when I went to check out the church our children would be attending while in college. Bill was ill, so I made the trip alone to meet our children there. I found them already seated with some of their college friends, so I slipped in beside my daughter and pretended to be invisible. I was only deceiving myself. I watched with pleasure as I saw my son and daughter interacting with those around them before the service started. Little people are always attracted to my daughter, so I thought nothing of it when the baby in the bench ahead held out her little stuffed bunny for Heather to take. I watched as the young people passed that bunny back and forth, but what I didn't see was that they were pulling a string before they gave it to each other. The bunny went up the line and back to Heather. Apparently, she thought I needed to "hold" the bunny also. I did! For a total of two seconds! Accompanied by a yelp, I threw that bunny so hard, it flew halfway across the church and hit a window. No harm was done except that the young people and the people behind me were left in convulsions of laughter.

Heather retrieved the bunny and gave it back to the child. She apologized saying, "Mom, I had no idea you'd do that. That bunny vibrates when you pull the cord."

Precisely. I didn't have this foreknowledge; therefore, when the bunny arrived in my hand, I was surprised it was all but alive. So much for playing low-key. I had hit all the high notes. I'm sure I will always be remembered as the lady who threw the rabbit.

Crash bars!

Another time, I went to a writer's conference. My arthritis had put me into a wheelchair, so I needed some big-time help. My daughter-in-law sweetly complied, and since we were running late, I said, "Hurry!" Hurry she did. I purposely chose the side door so we would not be center stage upon entering. So much for that! My daughter-in-law was not used to operating a wheelchair and proved a bit clumsy. She tried to hold open the double doors and push me in at the same time. She managed to rap the wheelchair against one door, overcorrect, and bash into the other door. Both doors had crash bars, and they became exactly that—crashing loudly as the wheelchair and her backside encountered them. The reverent atmosphere of the devotional was ruined as we "slipped in" as subtly as a train wreck.

Party Crashers

Don't you hate the times when you get overcommitted and find yourself trying to do too many things at the same time? We had company, whom we hated to leave, but we also needed to be at a function to honor a couple for something like an anniversary. My husband and I planned to just "slip in," pay our respects, sign the book, drop off our gift, and leave without much ado. We knew there would be so many people there we'd hardly be missed.

We sat for a bit with friends at a table that just happened to be next to where some entertainment was to take place. A sheet with holes in it for the men to put their noses into had been hung, and each wife was to go and identify her husband's nose. One of our friends just insisted that Bill go put his nose through to see if I would recognize it. That same friend had told his wife to look for the X he planned to draw on his nose just before he put it through the hole. We wanted to hold back and just watch. How I wish we had! As fate would have it, we had to participate. Bill should have known better, but when he saw me from his darkened side of the sheet, he wanted me to know it was him and snorted. The result? I screamed. No little quiet exit. Everyone present had their eyes on us. Puh-leeze! We explained to our company later about our delay.

Attention Please

Once I was kindly invited to an Amish friend's wedding. I was told the service would begin early, but that I could come anytime before noon. I hate going to weddings without my husband, but he had to work and planned to come later in the day. I arrived at eleven o'clock and found only horses and buggies, but no human beings. I knew the wedding was to be in the basement of the house, but I did not know which door I was to go in. As I stood there in my dilemma, a young man came out carrying a crying baby, so I asked him where to go.

He said, "See that door? You can go in there."

He had just come out that door, so it made sense to me. Only after I had opened the door and entered the darkness, did I realize I was on the side where only the men sat. It was too late to run. I quickly sized things up and realized I needed to make my way to the women's side. The only open route was down an aisle with men on both sides, passing within twelve inches of the preacher's nose and then right between the bride and groom, who sat facing each other.

No "slipping in" here. The crowd had already been there for a couple hours listening to the speaker drone on and on, when the door opened, letting in a lot of sunshine and a stranger. I felt like a butterfly dressed in my light lavender dress as I fluttered down through the rows of black- and navy-clad folks to find my place among the women.

The Lord knows I do not intend to draw attention to myself. I have looked long and hard in the Bible to try to find people or circumstances that relate to my life. It is wonderful to know you are in God's will, but sometimes, I just don't understand why (when I mean something for nothing but good) such embarrassing things happen. I suppose some hard-nosed folks would probably say, "It's because you're proud and God is bringing you down."

Whoa, most of the time, I feel the Lord has to spend way too much time lifting me up. He knows the thoughts and intents of our hearts. One of these days, I plan to not just be "slipping in" but entering the gates of Heaven with great joy and singing. I don't intend to just slip in, unobserved, but with boldness hurry up to the throne and cast my crown before Him.

CPSIA information can be obtained at www.ICGtesting.com
Printed in the USA
BVOW072306090412

287269BV00001B/2/P